Tornado and VxWorks
What's not in the Manual

1st Edition

Christof Wehner

2006

Dedicated to my grandmother, Elisabeth Blome, who died on July 20, 1999 after living for 101 Years. Remember that all technology we take for granted today was developed in the lifespan of a single human being!
Also dedicated to my wife, Juliane S.E. Wehner who bears with me throughout the times, good and not so good.

Title Picture ©2003 Christof Wehner and licensors. Portions courtesy of FORCE Computers, Inc.
Published by Books On Demand GmbH Printing Service, Germany
www.bod.de

Copyright © 2006 by Christof Wehner
All rights reserved.

The right of Christof Wehner to be identified as author of this work has been asserted in accordance with the Copyright, Designs and Patents Act, 1988

This book and any excerpts may not be copied without the express permission of the publisher and the author.

Typeset using TeX and LaTeX

ISBN 3-8334-4437-1

Contents

1 Introduction   1
    1.1 Demo Environment used for This Book 1
    1.2 Book Contents 1
    1.3 Conventions 2
    1.4 Copyrights and Trademarks 3

2 Basic Concepts & Overview   5
    2.1 Basic Terms 5
       2.1.1 Target and Host 5
    2.2 Real-time 5
    2.3 Determinism – or Predictability? 6
       2.3.1 Definition of Determinism 7
       2.3.2 Definition of Predictability 7
       2.3.3 Comparison 7
    2.4 Portability 7
    2.5 Development Strategies 8
       2.5.1 Target based Development 8
       2.5.2 Cross Development 8
    2.6 Layered Architecture 9
       2.6.1 Board Support Package — BSP 10
       2.6.2 Kernel and Architecture-dependent Code 10
       2.6.3 Application 11
    2.7 Host Support Package HSP 11
       2.7.1 Tool Sets and Tool Architecture 11
       2.7.2 Target based Tools 17
    2.8 Implementation of the Tool Set on the Different Hosts 18
       2.8.1 UNIX Hosts - Solaris (and — historically — HP/UX) 18
       2.8.2 Windows NT Hosts 18
       2.8.3 All Hosts 18
    2.9 Documentation 19
       2.9.1 Tornado User's Guide 19
       2.9.2 VxWorks Programmer's Guide 19
       2.9.3 VxWorks Network Programmer's Guide 19

	2.9.4	VxWorks Programmer's Reference	19
	2.9.5	Architecture-Supplement – Architecture-Specific Information	20
	2.9.6	Tornado API Guide	20
	2.9.7	Additional Documentation	20
	2.9.8	GNU toolset documentation	20
	2.9.9	Online Documentation	21

3 Setup 25
- 3.1 Installations 25
  - 3.1.1 Before You Start - Think first! 25
  - 3.1.2 Setting Up the Host 26
  - 3.1.3 Installing the BSP 27
- 3.2 What is Where – The Directory Structure 31
  - 3.2.1 *docs* directory 31
  - 3.2.2 *host* directory 31
  - 3.2.3 *setup* directory 31
  - 3.2.4 *share* directory 32
  - 3.2.5 *target* directory 32
  - 3.2.6 But There is Still More - *.wind* 36
  - 3.2.7 The Old Times — Before Tornado 36
- 3.3 Configuration Basics 36
  - 3.3.1 Configuration Tool & Project Workspace 36
  - 3.3.2 Rebuilding the Kernel 37
- 3.4 Different Goals, different Kernels 38
  - 3.4.1 Bootrom 38
  - 3.4.2 Kernel 39

4 Booting the Target 41
- 4.1 The bootrom 41
  - 4.1.1 The Parameters 41
  - 4.1.2 Bootrom Development – When and How 46
  - 4.1.3 Network Boot 48
  - 4.1.4 SCSI Boot 48
  - 4.1.5 Shared Memory Network 57
- 4.2 Kernel Boot 59
  - 4.2.1 Standard Kernel — *VxWorks* 59
  - 4.2.2 Standalone Kernel — *vxWorks.st* 60
  - 4.2.3 Rommable Kernels 60
- 4.3 Common Problems 60

5 Programming 63
- 5.1 Basic Concepts 63
  - 5.1.1 Compatibility, Porting 63
- 5.2 Programming to Debug 64
  - 5.2.1 Example Code 64
  - 5.2.2 Compiling The Code 65
  - 5.2.3 What happens when Downloading Code? 65
  - 5.2.4 When to link code 65
- 5.3 Debugging 66
  - 5.3.1 The *Crosswind* Debugger 66
  - 5.3.2 Choosing Your Debug Environment 66
- 5.4 C++ and VxWorks 69
  - 5.4.1 Wind Foundation Classes 69
  - 5.4.2 tools.h++ and Booch Classes 70
- 5.5 Starting and Running your Application 70
  - 5.5.1 Big Block - ONE package doing it All 70
  - 5.5.2 Startup Scripts 71
  - 5.5.3 Dynamically Loading Applications and Starting Them 71
  - 5.5.4 Usual Problems 72
- 5.6 Programming VME and PCI devices 72
  - 5.6.1 Bus Devices 73
  - 5.6.2 Programming Devices 77
- 5.7 VxWorks Additional Devices – Drivers 80
  - 5.7.1 The Driver Concept of VxWorks 80
- 5.8 Interrupts in VxWorks 85
  - 5.8.1 VMEbus Interrupts 86
  - 5.8.2 Interrupt Internals 88
  - 5.8.3 PCIbus Interrupts – What's the Difference? 89
  - 5.8.4 Emergency Interrupts – NMIs 90
- 5.9 Staying Portable 90
  - 5.9.1 Reasoning 90
  - 5.9.2 Considerations for staying Portable 91
  - 5.9.3 POSIX.x 95
  - 5.9.4 Conclusion 97

6 VxWorks Modules 99
- 6.1 How and Why does adding/removing Modules affect the Kernel Size? 99
  - 6.1.1 Background – Symbol Tables 99
  - 6.1.2 Linking the Modules 101
- 6.2 Basic Modules 101
  - 6.2.1 Networking 101
  - 6.2.2 SCSI 102
  - 6.2.3 Target Agent and Target Shell 102

CONTENTS

- 6.3 Optional Modules to add Functionality 102
  - 6.3.1 FTP Server 102
  - 6.3.2 NFS 102
  - 6.3.3 NFS Server 103
  - 6.3.4 Rlogin and Telnet 103
  - 6.3.5 SENS 103

7 Important BSP Information — 105
- 7.1 BSP Files 105
  - 7.1.1 Makefile 105
  - 7.1.2 config.h 107
  - 7.1.3 <BSP_NAME>.h 119
  - 7.1.4 sysSerial.c 120
  - 7.1.5 sysScsi.c 120
  - 7.1.6 sysVme.c 120
  - 7.1.7 sysLib.c 120
- 7.2 VxWorks System Files 122
  - 7.2.1 bootConfig.c 122
  - 7.2.2 usrConfig.c 122
  - 7.2.3 usrScsi.c, usrIde.c 122
  - 7.2.4 usrNetwork.c 122
  - 7.2.5 usrAppInit.c 123
- 7.3 Gathering Additional Information 123

8 Tailoring Your Setup to Your Needs — 125
- 8.1 Cleaning Up the Kernel Modules 125
- 8.2 Optimization 126
- 8.3 Profiling 128
  - 8.3.1 RTIlib – A Utility Library 129
  - 8.3.2 Coverage Analysis Tools 129
- 8.4 WindView to Enhance System Performance 129
  - 8.4.1 Instrumentation 129
  - 8.4.2 Modes 130
  - 8.4.3 Limitations 130
  - 8.4.4 Things To Do After Using WindView 131
- 8.5 Tailoring the System to your Application 131
  - 8.5.1 Application Structure 131
  - 8.5.2 Hardware Setup 132
  - 8.5.3 System Design 133

9 Troubleshooting VxWorks 135
- 9.1 Installation 135
- 9.2 Boot Process 135
  - 9.2.1 Shared Memory Network 135
  - 9.2.2 Download Issues 136
  - 9.2.3 General Networking Issues 136
- 9.3 Running the Target 136
  - 9.3.1 License Issues 136
  - 9.3.2 Other Topics while Developing or Running the Target System 137

A Important Defines and Modules 139
- A.1 VxWorks Modules 139
  - A.1.1 Compatibility Packages 139
  - A.1.2 ANSI C support – default 140
  - A.1.3 BootP support – default 140
  - A.1.4 BSD socket support – default 140
  - A.1.5 Cache Support – default 141
  - A.1.6 C++ support – default disabled 141
  - A.1.7 Wind Foundation Classes – add-on 141
  - A.1.8 CodeTest Utility Library — add-on 142
  - A.1.9 Pre-Tornado Debug Facilities – default disabled 142
  - A.1.10 The DEMO application – default disabled 142
  - A.1.11 File systems – default disabled 142
  - A.1.12 Additional Network Interfaces – default disabled 143
  - A.1.13 UNIX-compatible Environment Variables – default 143
  - A.1.14 Basic Exception Handling – default 143
  - A.1.15 Floating Point and GCC Floating Point Libraries – default .. 143
  - A.1.16 Formatted I/O – default 144
  - A.1.17 FTP Server – default disabled 144
  - A.1.18 WindView – add-on 144
  - A.1.19 The I/O System – default 145
  - A.1.20 The Object Module Loader – default disabled 145
  - A.1.21 Logging Facilities – default 145
  - A.1.22 Full Featured Memory Manager – default 145
  - A.1.23 MIB 2 Support – default disabled 145
  - A.1.24 MMU support Levels - default and add-on 146
  - A.1.25 Message Queues – default 146
  - A.1.26 Networking – default 146
  - A.1.27 NFS Support Packages – default disabled 147
  - A.1.28 Pipes – default 148
  - A.1.29 POSIX Support - default disabled 148
  - A.1.30 Remote Serial Connections - PPP – default disabled 148
  - A.1.31 PROXY networks – default disabled 148

- A.1.32 RAMdrv, A RAM disk driver – default disabled 149
- A.1.33 Remote Debugging – default disabled 149
- A.1.34 rlogin, allowing network access to your target – default disabled 149
- A.1.35 Remote Procedure Calls, RPC – default disabled 150
- A.1.36 Shell Security Package – default disabled 150
- A.1.37 Socket Select() package – default 150
- A.1.38 Different Semaphores – default 150
- A.1.39 Target based shell – default disabled 151
- A.1.40 Show Routines – default disabled 151
- A.1.41 Signal facility – default 151
- A.1.42 Serial Line IP Package – default disabled 151
- A.1.43 Shared Memory Network, Communication via a backplane bus – default 151
- A.1.44 Shared Memory Objects, VxMP – add-on 152
- A.1.45 SNMP Agent – add-on 152
- A.1.46 SPY, Task Monitoring Facility – default disabled 152
- A.1.47 Standalone Symbol table – default disabled 152
- A.1.48 Starting to do things right after booting, Startup Script – default disabled 152
- A.1.49 User-Readable Error states – default disabled 153
- A.1.50 Standard I/O – default 153
- A.1.51 STREAMS – add-on 153
- A.1.52 Software Floating Point – default disabled as of Tornado 2 . . 153
- A.1.53 Symbol Table – default disabled 154
- A.1.54 Task Hooks - default 154
- A.1.55 Task Variables – default 154
- A.1.56 TCP Debug Tools – default disabled 154
- A.1.57 Telnet Style Remote Login to the target system – default disabled 154
- A.1.58 TFTP Tools – default disabled 155
- A.1.59 Function Execution Time Measurement Library – default . . . 155
- A.1.60 Serial Devices – default 155
- A.1.61 Object Module Unloader – default 155
- A.1.62 Watchdogs – default 155
- A.1.63 WDB, the Wind DeBug Agent – default 156
- A.1.64 Zero Copying Sockets – default disabled 156
- A.1.65 New features with Tornado 2 – default disabled 156
- A.2 CPU Types 157
  - A.2.1 MC68000, MC68010, MC68020, MC68030, MC68040, MC68LC040, MC68060 – Motorola 680x0 Series 157
  - A.2.2 CPU32 – Motorola MC 68360 Series 157
  - A.2.3 SPARC, SPARClite – SUN Microsystems SPARC Architecture 158
  - A.2.4 I960CA, I960KA, I960KB, I960JX, I960HX – Intel i960 CPU Series 158

CONTENTS

A.2.5	R3000, R4000, R4000, R4650, MIPS – MIPS Processors . . .	158
A.2.6	AM29030, AM29200, AM29035 – AM29xxx Series	158
A.2.7	PPC601, PPC602, PPC603, PPC604, PPC403. PPC505, PPC740, PPC750, PPC860, PPCEC603 – Motorola/IBM/Apple PowerPC Series	158
A.2.8	I80386, I80486, I80X86 – Intel x86 Series	158
A.2.9	SIMSPARCSUNOS, SIMSPARCSOLARIS, SIMHPPAHPUX, SIMNT – VxWorks Simulator Pseudo-Processor Series	158

B Makefile Rules — A Short Introduction 159
B.1 Definitions And Rules 159
    B.1.1 Additional Standard Targets 160
    B.1.2 A Dependency Checker – *makedepend* 160
B.2 Example Codes 161
    B.2.1 Example *Makefile* 161
    B.2.2 rtc.h 162
    B.2.3 rtc.c 162
B.3 Compiler Options 163
    B.3.1 Compilation, Linking and Debugging 163
    B.3.2 Optimization 164

C Building you own Toolchain 165
C.1 Getting the Files 165
C.2 Rebuilding the Complete Toolchain 166
    C.2.1 Building the Utility Toolchain 166
    C.2.2 Rebuilding *gcc* 166

D Pointers to Different Internet Sites 167
D.1 Specifications And References Online 167
D.2 Online VxWorks Pages And General Real-time Related Information . 168
D.3 Programming Tools Online 168
D.4 Newsgroups 169
D.5 This Book 169

Bibliography

[Boo95] Grady Booch. *Object-Oriented Analysis and Design with Applications, 2nd Ed.* The Benjamin/Cummings Publishing Company, Inc., 1995.

[Dav93] Stephen R. Davis. *C++ Programmer's Companion — Designing, Testing and Debugging.* Addison Wesley, 1993.

[FSF99a] Free Software Foundation FSF. *GDB, The GNU Debugger Version 4.17.* Free Software Foundation, 1999.

[FSF99b] Free Software Foundation FSF. *GNU Toolkit User's Guide*, chapter GCC User's Guide. Free Software Foundation, 1999.

[Gal95] Bill O. Gallmeister. *POSIX.4.* O'Reilly, 1995.

[MW94] Merriam-Webster. *Webster's new encyclopedic dictionary.* Black Dog & Leventhal Publishers Inc., 1994.

[Tal91] Andrew Oram & Steve Talbott. *Managing Projects with Make (A Nutshell Book), 2nd Ed.* O'Reilly, 1991.

[WRS97] Wind River Systems WRS. Device drivers training class. Class, 1997.

[WRS99a] Wind River Systems WRS. *Tornado 2.0 API Programmer's Guide.* Wind River Systems, 1999.

[WRS99b] Wind River Systems WRS. *Tornado 2.0 Programmer's Guide*, chapter 5.5 — Wind Foundation Classes. Wind River Systems, 1999.

[WRS99c] Wind River Systems WRS. *Tornado 2.0 Programmer's Guide*, chapter 4.7 – The Target Server File System: TSFS. Wind River Systems, 1999.

[WRS99d] Wind River Systems WRS. *Tornado 2.0 User's Guide – UNIX Version*, chapter 2.3 – The Tornado Host Environment, page 20 ff. Wind River Systems, 1999.

[WRS99e] Wind River Systems WRS. *Tornado 2.0 User's Guide – Windows Version*, chapter 2 – Setup and Startup. Wind River Systems, 1999.

[WRS99f] Wind River Systems WRS. *Tornado Getting Started Guide*. Wind River Systems, 1999.

[WRS99g] Wind River Systems WRS. *VxWorks 5.4 Network Programmer's Guide*, chapter 4.7 – ARP and Proxy ARP for transparent subnets, page 84 ff. Wind River Systems, 1999.

[WRS99h] Wind River Systems WRS. *VxWorks 5.4 Network Programmer's Guide*, chapter 3.5 – Shared Memory Network on the Backplane, page 40 ff. Wind River Systems, 1999.

[WRS99i] Wind River Systems WRS. *VxWorks 5.4 Programmer's Guide*, chapter 3.9 – I/O System Internal Structure, page 140 ff. Wind River Systems, 1999.

[WRS99j] Wind River Systems WRS. *VxWorks 5.4 Programmer's Guide*, chapter 2.5 - Interrupt Service Code, page 85 ff. Wind River Systems, 1999.

[WRS99k] Wind River Systems WRS. *VxWorks 5.4 Programmer's Guide*, chapter 4 – Local File Systems, page 175 ff. Wind River Systems, 1999.

[WRS99l] Wind River Systems WRS. *VxWorks 5.4 Reference Manual*. Wind River Systems, 1999.

List of Figures

2.1	Principle of Cross-Development System – Target and Host	6
2.2	Layered Architecture – Principle	10
2.3	Example for the UNIX Tornado Interface	12
2.4	Example for the NT Tornado IDE	15
2.5	The UNIX version of the Tornado 1.0 Configuration Tool	16
2.6	The Project Tool's User Interface and functionality, here showing the VxWorks Selection view	23
2.7	The Project Tool's User Interface and functionality, here showing the BSP File Selection view	24
3.1	Library Update Example	30
3.2	*target* subtree of the installation	33
3.3	Addition to *rules.bsp* to allow uncompressed, rommable kernel	40
4.1	Example output for `help` command at the bootprompt	43
4.2	Excerpt from */etc/inetd.conf*	47
4.3	Sample entry from */etc/ethers*	47
4.4	Excerpt from *usrScsi.c*: Default SCSI Configuration	51
4.5	Excerpt from *usrScsi.c*: Our example SCSI Configuration	52
4.6	Principle of PROXY Network Routing	58
4.7	Principle of IP Network Routing	59
5.1	Example of Debug Output Code	67
5.2	Excerpt from *usrConfig.c*, User Application start code	70
5.3	Code excerpt from *usrApplInit.c* – where application startup code should be inserted	71
5.4	Accessing Addresses on Bus Systems - Principle	76
5.5	Example for an ideal Interrupt Service Routine, ISR	86

List of Tables

2.1 List of the UNIX binary utilities, also available in Windows. 13
4.1 Standard Boot Devices for PowerCore-6604 42
4.2 *usrScsi.c* SCSI Default Setup 49
5.1 Example for a VME mapping – Default Setup for PowerCore 75
6.1 Symbol Types in Object Modules 100

Preface

The Tornado IDE and its companion real time operating system VxWorks have come a long way. Starting out in the 80's as a set of libraries for other real time kernels, VxWorks version 5.0's WIND kernel has become the basis for the world's predominant real time operating system.
    I got into the story at stage 5.0.2, working at the university and then progressed through the different versions while working in the Technical Support team at FORCE Computers. Seeing VxWorks grow from just libraries plus kernel, built on a UNIX system using *make* (which required a lot of experience and knowledge about where and how UNIX stored files) to a full IDE with a helpful interface that adds the background knowledge about which things requires what has been quite impressing. However some knowledge of what is below might still help in working with the overall system. And that is what I intended to share when I started out on this book years ago. By now, 2 versions of Tornado later, I finally have managed to finish this endeavour.
    I hope you will enjoy reading this book and also get some useful information from it. Let me know!

Thank You

There are some people who helped me get the book out who should not go unnamed.
    First, Torsten Pierro for helping me to get my grammar straight, Ulrike Müller who provided the basis for the title picture (thanks to FORCE Computers).
    Second, my managers at FORCE who let me go on with this project - Alexander Keck, Achim Apel and Günter Graf.
    And, most of all, Juliane.

Chapter 1

Introduction

Tornado 1.x, 2.x and VxWorks, the operating system "below" Tornado, have gained more and more acceptance in the market place. There are some reasons for this phenomenon:

More and more companies move from their proprietary operating system to a standard system. This helps them center their resources on their core goal, to develop applications based on something more general. The same trend has been true for the hardware they base their systems on. Today, more and more projects are based on slightly customized platforms using standard operating systems.

So, the companies concentrate on their area of expertise and make use of the operating system's vendor's expertise for the layers below.

Additionally, VxWorks became more and more successful *because* of its portability. Moving to a different platform is not as difficult to achieve as before.

1.1 Demo Environment used for This Book

This book is based on Tornado 2, with a major focus on UNIX. As the lower layers are identical between UNIX and Windows, this is no real problem; where applicable and desirable, the MS Windows versions are discussed separately.

To install Tornado, you will need an installation key. This key is delivered as part of your package; you will also gain access to WindSurf, Wind River's online support. Browse around, there is a lot of interesting information buried there!

1.2 Book Contents

The book mainly focuses on backgrounds and where to get additional information, while also covering the concepts below. In addition, there are many things that were found to be unclear or difficult to understand which could result in common pitfalls in tech support for VxWorks.

This results in the following general structure:

- Basic Concepts talking about the internal architecture and other basic information
- Setup and options installing VxWorks plus the issues you might encounter after installation
- Booting the target system, and configuring the target for some boot options that are not very common
- Programming using VxWorks, what to do and how to debug applications and low level code. Also how to keep your code reusable for future applications
- VxWorks modules gives an overview over some of the commonly used modules, what can and what cannot be done
- BSP Information shows what is hidden where, and how to configure your BSP to achieve the configuration you need
- Tailoring the system shows how to make the overall system and application software design achieve its goals and also how to find possible areas that may create problems
- Troubleshooting finally gives pointers to troubleshooting information found throughout the book
- The Appendices then show the modules and their enabling/disabling in *configAll.h*, and more information of that might be of interest.

1.3 Conventions

Throughout this document, the following conventions will be used:

- `source code` will be written using Courier fonts.
- *Commands* are written in slanted font.
- *File names and paths* are written in italics, using the UNIX convention of '/' to separate directories. Tornado's Windows C compilers and C libraries are built on *gcc* and accept this convention anyway, so there should not be any problems caused by this.
- Bold faces denote **function_names()** in the text.

1.4 Copyrights and Trademarks

VxWorks, Tornado and Wind River Systems are registered trademarks of Wind River Systems, Inc.

Any other named trademark or product may be a registered trademark of the respective owner.

Source and demo code is part of this publication without any warranty of being useful or correct, even though we did our best to make sure that all code was tested prior to being published. The code may also be owned by other individuals or companies without explicit notice.

Chapter 2

Basic Concepts & Overview

This chapter discusses basic concepts for real time systems. Later we will start discovering how these concepts are used in VxWorks and how they influence the operating system.

2.1 Basic Terms

First of all, let us clear up some basic terms which will be used very often in this book.
The terms Tornado and VxWorks are used in this book side by side. Why?
Well, VxWorks is the real time kernel plus libraries and drivers that runs software that is developed using the Tornado IDE. VxWorks is the kernel plus the API set plus some additional software tools. So, what it boils down to is that one without the other proves pretty useless. Tornado is the overall integrated packge plus the IDE. What counts for the end application, is VxWorks, not the IDE. But the IDE definitely helps a lot...!

2.1.1 Target and Host

The term target refers to the system you are developing for; this is the system the code is *targeted* for.
Compared to that, the system the development takes place on is referred to as the host. The host hosts the development system. The principle of this setup is shown in figure 2.1 on page 6.

2.2 Real-time

What is real-time? Most people think, real-time always means very, very fast. That is not correct!
The German norms body, DIN, has a simple definition for real-time which hits the point right on:

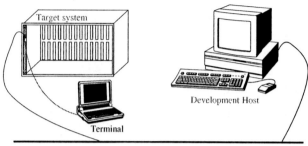

Figure 2.1: Principle of Cross-Development System – Target and Host

<u>Real-time</u> means that a maximum time can be calculated in which the system will respond to an event at the latest.

This means, hours, even days will be ok, as long as there is a maximum time computable! What does it mean for everyday real-time applications? Simple: if your car's brakes are operated using a real-time O/S (around the time this is written, that is improbable, but chances are growing!), then a maximum time can be calculated when, after pressing the brake, your car will actually slow down unless something's seriously wrong.

Normally, this timeframe is somewhere in the msec or μsec timeframe. And that is the reason why it is fairly often mistaken to mean fast. It does not, even though it normally makes sure that most tasks are taken care of very fast.

So, being fast is the result of being real-time, not the other way around! Anyway, real-time means a lot more for the end user.

2.3 Determinism – or Predictability?

To achieve real-time behavior in a system, you have to have an exact state machine. Otherwise, the maximum time cannot be computed because the state changes are not predictable. An example for this behavior is UNIX. Here, if you start enough processes, the behavior and the time when your process will run may become unpredictable. But be sure to run this test on an old version of UNIX. Today's implementations have added a lot to get around these types of problems. Anyway, they are a

2.4. PORTABILITY

lot bigger and more complex at the core than any real-time operating system. And, as they are doing so many additional things, they are only usable for 'soft' real-time applications.

2.3.1 Definition of Determinism

Determinism means, according to [MW94], *"a doctrine, that acts of the will, natural events, or social changes [or changes in general] are determined by preceding processes"*.

This, transferred in to normal terms, means that, for the same set of inputs, you get the same result.

2.3.2 Definition of Predictability

Predictability means, according to [MW94], *"declarable in advance, foretold on the basis of observation, experience or scientific reasoning"* (adapted from the definition for "predict, *vt*").

This means that by understanding you can predict the result of whatever event takes place.

2.3.3 Comparison

So, they both are similar but are not exactly the same. For real-time systems, they both are important.

Determinism is the basis for the predictability of real-time operating systems, though. Predictability only means it may be predicted; determinism means that the result is set in stone, thus making the system's behavior fully predictable.

The story goes that, when the very first UNIX machines were scrapped after many, many years, some of the very first programs created on these machines were still running because they never got enough time to finish. This might prove quite a problem in the case of the brakes of your car...

2.4 Portability

Portability is a big issue within today's development community. The big question that is answered by being portable is - what if my current development base cannot deliver the performance I need?

In this case, the answer is simple - move to a new one which *does* deliver the necessary performance. If you built your application on a proprietary system running on proprietary hardware, this is not easily achieved. If you are using commercial systems on commercial hardware, maybe even your hardware vendor can help directly.

If your application was designed with portability in mind, a recompile plus extensive tests to find any designed-in non-portable features should do. Be careful in this area. For example, `short` is a data type people love to use. But is it really the same size (16 bit) on both PowerPC and 680x0 systems? In this case, it is, but the future will show that these habit-defined names might change (`int`, `char` etc. are ANSI C defined (For instance, `short` is not).

So, a standardized API together with a clean abstraction-layer may not cut development cost in the beginning, but at the latest when moving on to a different environment or hardware.

There is a specific chapter in this book, discussing ways to make code portable, and why this is desirable. See chapter 5.9 on page 90.

2.5 Development Strategies

For developing real-time systems, there are currently two different approaches which both have their merits. We will discuss both of them in the following few lines.

2.5.1 Target based Development

In this case, the development is completely executed on the system you want to use for the final deployment.

The advantage of this approach is that you do not need extra resources like a development host or a network or other direct communication means. This strategy also yields the advantage of not needing additional hardware after the deployment. Normally, after development, you strip the deployment system down to the bare bones it needs to be able to run in the final application. Compilers, development environment and all additional tools are removed – this all costs money and resources such as disk space, memory space and additional hardware!

The disadvantage of the approach is that, after removing the development environment for deployment, you have no real way left to correct things on the target system. So, if something goes wrong or does not behave as expected, you need to re-install everything you need to continue development.

Additionally, the footprint of the development system on the target system is fairly big - it is all down there.

2.5.2 Cross Development

Cross-development is today's buzz word. In addition, it has become kind of fashionable.

2.6. LAYERED ARCHITECTURE

What is Cross Development?

Cross development means that you are building your application code on your favorite platform using your favorite editor and development tools, then compile on the host and download your application code to your target system to try it out there, on your target system. So, the term cross-development means development across operating systems and, usually but not necessarily, processor architectures.

Cross development is the alternative. Most vendors who offer target based development systems, today also offer cross-development solutions in addition to their native development environments. So what is the benefit here?

Comparison to Target-Based Development

In the first place, you get an a lot smaller footprint on the target system. And during development it will already be very much like the deployment system. So, less surprising behaviors are to be expected when deploying.

Second, you can run the development tools on your favorite, well-known development system. It is available for PCs and UNIX, so you do not have to learn a completely new environment plus whatever editor comes with the operating system.

Sounds great! Are there any downsides?

Well, there are always downsides these days.

You need a connection to your target. So, a network or a serial line (networks are a lot better due to their higher throughput) are necessary. In addition, you need the development system as well, and this is not necessarily an inexpensive solution.

2.6 Layered Architecture

A clean architecture with clear APIs is one of the most important features of a modern operating system. This becomes extremely important if the operating system is used for real-time applications.

To attain the additional benefits of having a good chance of porting applications from one platform to another, a layered approach which isolates every layer better from the very bottom hardware helps a great deal in achieving this goal. With VxWorks, a three-layered architecture isolates the application software from the full hardware. The O/S still allows direct access by bypassing the layers – but there are numerous tools to make life easier in many applications. So, first of all consider going through the operating system to remain portable. More information on this issue can also be found in chapter 5 on page 63.

In the following the different layers and their contents are discussed.

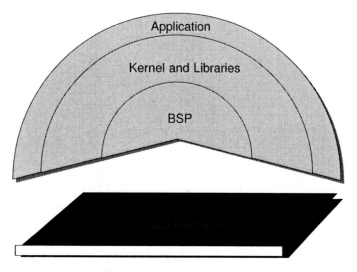

Figure 2.2: Layered Architecture – Principle

2.6.1 Board Support Package — BSP

The board support package is the glue between the architecture - dependent code and the actual hardware. It enables the same kernel to run on different board types. So for example the kernel only has to exist in a PowerPC 603 specific version and can run on all different vendors' boards based on a PowerPC 603 without having to be recreated for each and every one of them. The board support package delivers drivers for many board-specific components plus all the small helper functions which depend on the actual specifics like VMEbus access (**sysBusToLocalAdrs()** and **sysBusTas()**) and others.

We will see more of this in the back of the book. Note though that these functions are defined in the BSP and delivered in source. So you can also change them to mirror your specific environment or, even better, make this information available to others in your development team!

2.6.2 Kernel and Architecture-dependent Code

The general API libraries and the kernel are running on top of the BSP and are delivered in an architecture-specific package. They need to reach out into the BSP for timer functions etc., but for all general functions, the interfaces are defined in this library.

The kernel itself is not board-specific due to its microkernel architecture. All additional functionality is delivered in additional plug-in modules which allow for a scal-

2.7. HOST SUPPORT PACKAGE HSP

able, extensible build of your system. Add what you need. What you do not need — throw out!

2.6.3 Application

The application is placed on top of this layer. This way your application normally does not need to know about the specifics of the board you are using, it is all hidden from it through BSP and API.

For some special tasks a direct access to the hardware or the BSP may be necessary. This should be done in a very limited and encapsulated way to enable easier porting at a later time. This can be achieved by encapsulating the hardware accesses in more general functions. These functions then should be placed in a separate file which is named according to the hardware it belongs to. You can find more information in chapter 5.9 on page 90.

2.7 Host Support Package HSP

The host support package consists of the cross-compilers, linker and additional tools which depend on the host's architecture and operating system. The tool chains are available for almost all UNIX systems and MS Windows in its 32bit flavors.

2.7.1 Tool Sets and Tool Architecture

For VxWorks, the standard toolchain delivered consists of the GNU tools *gcc*[1], the *binutils*[2] etc. in their respective cross-compiling versions. These specific tools are built and maintained by RedHat daughter Cygnus Inc., a company specialized in maintaining the GNU tools for customers who need a consistent support and porting level for the GNU tools.

These tools create the development side of VxWorks/Tornado. You can find a whole arrangement of different tools for your host to help you develop your application. In general, many of these tools follow the lines of UNIX development tools plus a <target architecture> postfix, like *ccppc*. This means, *cc* (i.e. C Compiler) for the target architecture PowerPC (*ppc*). Figure 2.1 contains a list of the usual set of utilities. The tools are for instance run when you choose "Build kernel" in the Build Menu.

The connection to the target is managed through *wdb*, the **Wind Debug Agent** running on the target system and a Target Server program running on the host side. This target server offers plug-in docks for additional applications to use it. This is

---

[1] *gcc* stands for GNU *cc*, the GNU C Compiler in the version shipped with VxWorks. As of version 3, *gcc* stands for GNU Compiler Collection as many more compilers have been integrated. See *http://www.gnu.org/gcc* for more information.

[2] The *binutils* is a package consisting of all the little helpers you need for dealing with binaries, i.e. object code. They include programs like *ld*, *ar* etc.

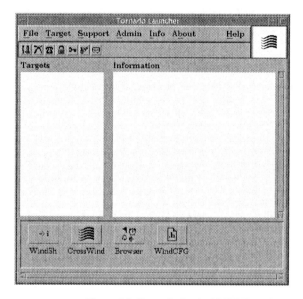

Figure 2.3: Example for the UNIX Tornado Interface

used by Tornado tools like *windsh, browser* and *crosswind* which are either called from the IDE for Windows or from the UNIX *launch* program. See figure 2.3 for a picture of *launch*!

The GNU Compilers

Why use the GNU compilers, is a commonly asked question. Well, there are several answers.

- One, they are free. If you obey the Gnu General Public License, you are free to use these tools for your development and more. If you need professional support, RedHat offers it. See appendix D for online contact information.

- Two, they are easy-to-configure and have built-in cross-compile support. This is a major point for using them in this environment. Additionally, though this may not have been a major point in choosing them, you can always download a newer version from the Internet and rebuild them yourself. Appendix C gives a short overview about what is necessary to rebuild them. But — no guarantees and do not quote me!

2.7. HOST SUPPORT PACKAGE HSP

Tool Name	Tool Function
cc	C and C++ Compiler
cpp	C Preprocessor
ld	Linker
as	Assembler
gasp	Assembly Preprocessor
ar	Archive Utility allows to manipulate object modules in libraries (*libxxx.a*)
nm	NaMe - displays the symbol table of object modules or archives.
objcopy	converts an object file to another, with the possibility to change formats, e.g. create S Records etc.
objdump	displays information about a given object file
ranlib	updates a library's Table of contents
size	displays the sizes of the different segments of an object module
strings	extracts and displays the strings contained in a binary file.
strip	removes symbols from an object module (obsolete - use objcopy!)
c++filter	converts C++ mangled symbols into readable text.

Table 2.1: List of the UNIX binary utilities, also available in Windows.

- Three, Internet development and support is a lot better than most people believe. Because there are so many users out there, and the compilers and tools are delivered in source code, the users are fairly willing to find where the error they experience comes from and fix it themselves and later transferring this solution to the community. This works very well, especially in the case of widely used tools like compilers. And, posting your question to a newsgroup normally yields answers within 24 hours. Something one cannot say for every form of support media...

Other Toolchains

In addition, Wind River daughter company Diab Data and Greenhills Software offer cross-compiling tools which may be used in conjunction with VxWorks[3]. The standard variant though is the GNU toolchain as delivered. Companies building board support packages normally also only use this toolchain for their development[4]. The other toolchains may, however, deliver better code generation and compilation options. So, you may want to know that they are there out there. Keep in mind you may need to change the Makefiles as well.

---
[3] Contact Information on their web sites as shown in appendix D
[4] This has changed with the appearance of Tornado 2.2. Now, both Diab and GNU are delivered in the package. They deliver compatible code, promises WindRiver.

Additional Host Tools

In addition to the GNU tools, Tornado delivers a lot more. This means the Launcher for UNIX and the IDE for Windows and all the tools to start from it.

- Target Server

    In some ways, a target server also is a host tool. This program manages the access to a target system and runs on the host side. So it can also be called a host tool.

- Registry

    The registry is a means of providing access to target servers spread out over a network or running on a local host. It offers the advantage of having an overview over the currently available target systems plus additional information. Today, it may be called a directory service.

    Here all target servers started somewhere in a group *register* that they exist, and then, the other programs can use the registry to find out how to contact a specific target server.

- Launch – UNIX toolchain

    The Launcher offers a real time look at all target servers registered in a given registry host. Additionally, by selecting a target server, it displays additional information and allows the starting of the different Tornado tools for a specific target.

    In the launcher, the user may select a target, view additional information on the target and then *launch* tools to work with the target system. The window is shown on page 12.

- MS Windows IDE

    In addition to the launcher's abilities the MS Windows IDE offers a coloring source code editor and menu-driven access to Make. There are other additions, but these are the main highlights. Manual access to the command line to run e.g. *make* is still possible. So, for UNIX lovers, the familiar tools are also available.

- WindSh

    WindSh is the standard user shell for Vxworks. It runs on the host system and connects to the target system through the target server. It includes a C command interpreter, allowing direct execution of C functions. Additionally, it also offers a TCL mode which gives access to many calls from the TCL API.

2.7. HOST SUPPORT PACKAGE HSP

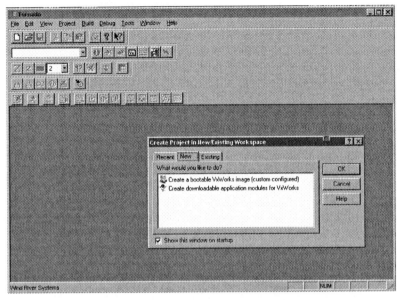

Figure 2.4: Example for the NT Tornado IDE

- Browser

    The browser allows a real-time look at a lot of information on the target system, like used/free memory, task table, object information and more. Here you can also select a refresh rate.

- Crosswind

    In principle Crosswind is an interface with added functions to gdb, the GNU DeBugger. It offers a GUI interface for source level debugging, even of interrupt service routines in system debug mode.

- Configuration Tool

    The configuration tool allows easy, visual setup of the target configuration with regard to VxWorks features. In Tornado 2, Windows Edition, it is integrated into the IDE.

    This works in the following way: a line is added to *config.h*, pointing to an additional header file which first #undefines all features and then #defines the features as needed. These features and some more can also be set up in the general configuration file, *.../target/config/all/configAll.h*. The standard way

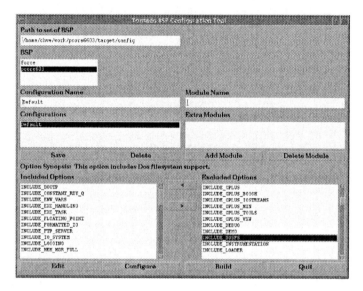

Figure 2.5: The UNIX version of the Tornado 1.0 Configuration Tool

for changes like these to be made should be to make changes to *config.h*. This ensures that these changes apply to this specific configuration instead of all configurations being created on the respective server! Make sure you only use ONE of these methods, not both! For a more detailed description of the different modules, see chapter A.1 on page 139.

With the release of Tornado 2's Project Tool this tool has become obsolete.

- Project Tool

  The Project Tool is one of the additions which comes with Tornado 2. It is a great help when working in environments with different setups, like developing an application which will run on multiple, similar processor boards with different tasks and configurations.

- Additional unsupported Tools delivered

  These are additional tools which are or have been used at Wind River and have been added to the distribution for the end user.

2.7. HOST SUPPORT PACKAGE HSP

- *shadow*

    shadow may be used to create local trees without directly accessing the source installation tree; but the installation tree may be kept in a read-only mode.

- *mangen*

    mangen is a tool which, when following the Wind River specification, allows the user to directly create UNIX man command compatible documentation from source files. This tool can be very helpful in development environments, because the additional step of creating documentation is unnecessary under these circumstances. For MS Windows, the tool has become obsolete; but anyway, it may be of interest to people who need to have in-code documentation and need to extract it.

    The tool disappeared as of Tornado 2.0. There is a successor called *refgen* that allows to generate documentation in HTML format.

- *mkmk*

    mkmk is a tool to create Makefiles which was used in versions of VxWorks prior to 5.3. So you can safely ignore it.

- *mpp*

    mpp created Makefiles from the file MakeSkel in VxWorks prior to version 5.3. Again, it can safely be ignored.

- *mofset*

    mofset is a tool to extract structures and union type definitions from standard C headers. It creates definitions for the respective offsets which may be used in assembler code afterwards.

2.7.2 Target based Tools

In addition to the host based tool set using *wdb*, VxWorks still has the old, 5.2 style tool set. There are basically two additional parts: *gdb* or *crosswind* still have the additional interface allowing to connect to the tRdbTask. It is started when selecting #define INCLUDE_RDB plus #defineing INCLUDE_CONFIGURATION_5_2 in *configAll.h* and rebuilding the kernel. This is not a very helpful addition, as it does not offer any additional capabilities compared to the *wdb* way of doing things.

That is the reason why WindRiver has removed RDB from Tornado 2. It is not a loss.

The real addition, especially for driver development and in the early stages of development of new applications and BSPs, is the target based shell. For example, when developing network drivers, using the *windsh* approach is slightly too early - there is no network connection available at this point in time! And, serial connections are fairly slow. So, why not go for this target based shell allowing direct, terminal-based access to the target system?

You can do runtime checks on variables, start functions, anything you can do in *windsh*, you can do here (with regard to C functions; development for the target shell has been dropped, so no TCL support is available!).

2.8 Implementation of the Tool Set on the Different Hosts

Tornado host tools come in two different types with many similarities and many dissimilarities. In general, these toolsets are called Tornado.

2.8.1 UNIX Hosts - Solaris (and — historically — HP/UX)

UNIX users normally already have picked their preferred editor, shell etc. So, Tornado for UNIX does not deliver these additional tools integrated.

The upside is that you are not forced to use any specific tool and can remain in your favorite environment.

The downside is that integration is not very high in this environment. Tornado for UNIX offers direct point-and-click access to all visual tools as delivered. But you may still have to compile your BSP yourselves using GNU *make*. UNIX *make* will complain about the *Makefiles*, so make sure you are using GNU *make* as delivered!

Note, that HP/UX is no longer a supported host environment.

2.8.2 Windows NT Hosts

Here, the level of integration is a lot higher than in the UNIX version. An integrated development environment (IDE) is delivered which allows menu-driven access to all necessary tools.

The upside is that integration is very nice and makes life a lot easier for beginners.

On the downside, this means that making any other customizations mean a lot more work.

2.8.3 All Hosts

Anyway, for both versions, the TCL API is documented in [WRS99a] and allows for customizations; also almost all command-line tools are delivered in both variants to allow for manual changes.

But, be very careful in this area — always create backups before trying out anything. Otherwise, the only way back may be a complete reinstall...

2.9 Documentation

A major part in working with operating systems, especially when writing software based on any operating system, is the documentation delivered with it. VxWorks comes with a whole lot of documentation which may or may not be used, depending on the goals of the user. In addition, VxWorks installations come with online versions of some of the different manuals.

Up-to-date versions of them can be retrieved from *http://www.windriver.com* in the Windsurf area which is restricted to maintenance customers.

In the following part, the manuals and their value for the respective groups admin, developer and user will be discussed.

2.9.1 Tornado User's Guide

This part of the documentation is intended to introduce the user to the tools that make up Tornado. It comes in different versions for UNIX and Windows, respectively.

It should be read by any person working with Tornado. There are several useful hints in it as well as basic information on the system.

2.9.2 VxWorks Programmer's Guide

This is the programmer's documentation. It can prove very useful once you know what you are doing.

At the end, you will also find documentation for the additional tools delivered with VxWorks that are not part of the GNU toolset.

It should be read by any developer working with VxWorks. The very first part is of interest also for people who want to understand more about how Tornado and VxWorks work.

2.9.3 VxWorks Network Programmer's Guide

This book has been moved from a section in the general Programmer's Guide into a separate book when the END/MUX networking model became standard for VxWorks. It holds a lot of information about the networking stack, supported protocols and how to program it.

The book is a must for everyone doing more than just downloading information over the network.

2.9.4 VxWorks Programmer's Reference

This is *the* manual for the programmer. It contains all manual pages for both functions and libraries as well as some generic BSP functions. For specific BSP functions, see page 21 for the online BSP documentation.

This manual is a must for any person programming with VxWorks.

2.9.5 Architecture-Supplement – Architecture-Specific Information

The architecture supplement is a must-read for every one who intends to do low-level development. It is also of high interest to everyone who intends to create protable software in order to avoid using architecture-specific features or in order to encapsulate them properly.

2.9.6 Tornado API Guide

This manual describes the TCL API of Tornado. It will prove a real help for anyone who wants to make extensions to the GUI tools. But not for programmers wanting to create target side code.

2.9.7 Additional Documentation

Some additional information is available in the smaller leaflets that come with VxWorks. Especially important was the ELAN license manager manual for Tornado 1. Make sure you keep it handy if you are still running Tornado 1!

Also, look through the other documents like Customer Support User's Guide, Release Notes and so on in order to get a good overview over what is available and what may be needed in the future.

2.9.8 GNU toolset documentation

The manuals contain the full printouts of all documentation delivered with the GNU toolset. It will prove a real help for any programmer who tries to tweak the compiler into doing exactly what he wants it to do.

There are three manuals in the Tornado 2 documentation set. Make sure to get a quick overview of them:

GNU Make User's Guide: GNU make is the version of *make* run as part of Tornado. As there are many options and dependencies, this book may prove of interest to people who need to build complex objects. For everyday life, appendix B on page 159 may be enough. If you need more, this is the place to look!

GDB (The GNU DeBbugger) User's Guide: GDB is the debugger basis run as engine of CrossWind. This is a book to at least browse through if you are planning serious development. Probably, while working with CrossWind, a closer look will be necessary.

2.9. DOCUMENTATION

GNU Toolkit Documentation: This book holds the documentation for all other GNU tools used in Tornado. Browse through it to find the information sources in case you need them in the future.

2.9.9 Online Documentation

VxWorks and Tornado come with a wealth of online documentation. Originally, they were all UNIX *man* pages; with the following convention:

- <function_name> for normal functions
- <BSPname>_<function_name> for BSP-specific functions.

With Tornado 1.x, these have been moved into the Wind Manual Tool for UNIX (*windman*); the Windows version is available in Windows Help format. These have the huge advantage that they are searchable.

As of Tornado 2, the manuals come in HTML format, readable by all standard web browsers. Better and easier to use.

BSP documentation

Of course, most BSPs do not only come with the basic set of functions as defined by VxWorks.

The BSP documentation describes installation of additional components, switch settings, boot processes and things as important as the memory map. Examples for additional functions are additions for flash memory, LEDs, 7 segment display, DMA copies from and to VME etc. Be sure to read these docs thoroughly.

Tornado 1: The additional functions can be found searching for the BSP name in the *target/man/* hierarchy of the Tornado 1 installation.

Tornado 2: Tornado 2 gave us the pages in HTML format. Normally, they can be found in the online documentation, named as the BSP directory.

Later, man pages were re-introduced in a text-formatted version.

Printing TROFF format Manual Pages on Solaris

Additionally, older BSP's main documentation pages describing the configuration of the board to be able to run VxWorks plus a general description of features supported came in the file *target.nr* in the BSP directory. The man-formatted version of the file is in *$(WIND_BASE)/target/man/man1/<BSP_NAME>.1* in *troff* format.

All these pages can be prepared for printing using *troff*. First, you need to copy the file *wrs.an* from *$(WIND_BASE)/target/man* to the BSP directory. Then, the command for Solaris is as follows:

```
% troff -man -Tpost target.nr|/usr/openwin/lib/lp/postscript/dpost|lp
```

This will send the pages to the system's default printer in PostScript format.

Viewing the *man* pages

The pages can be viewed using the UNIX command *man*. Additionally, a free PC version is available on several FTP servers. One of them, holding a distribution on the GNU toolset is referenced in appendix D.3, page 168.

2.9. DOCUMENTATION

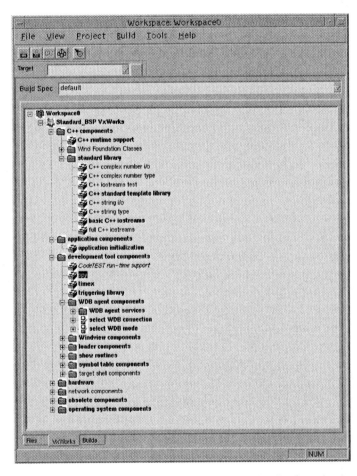

Figure 2.6: The Project Tool's User Interface and functionality, here showing the VxWorks Selection view

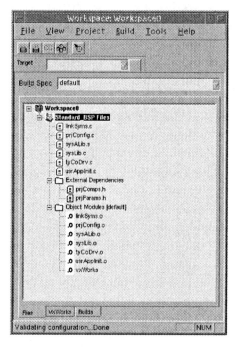

Figure 2.7: The Project Tool's User Interface and functionality, here showing the BSP File Selection view

Chapter 3

Setup

The system setup can be divided into two parts. First, the installation itself with regard to what is installed where and how things are installed.

The second part is the system configuration. There are many parameters which can be adjusted and changed to meet different needs.

3.1 Installations

The installation of an operating system is always a difficult task. For VxWorks though, the installation itself is fairly simple. The difficult part is to decide how to set up the installation tree depending on the future users of this tree.

3.1.1 Before You Start - Think first!

The main question is "What do you want to achieve with the installation?". Depending on the answer, there are different approaches to the "Installation Problem".

There are several possible setups which need to be discussed, depending on the different goals.

- Application Development

    For application development, people normally do not need access to the source tree other than using the include files (i.e. read the *.../target/h* directory). So, the best way is to keep the startup and installation files on a central server with only read access for the users.

- Driver Development

    For driver development, VxWorks allows for a similar setup as for the application development. As you do not need any additional rights, the cleanest way is to stay along those lines.

The only real change may be that a MODULE ID may need to be added to the file .../*target/h/vwModNum.h* if you want to enable the usage of `errno` and **printErr()** for your modules. This may also be a good choice when creating applications containing different modules.

- BSP Development

    This is a different issue. As the BSPs need to be added to the standard tree, at least part of this tree needs to be kept local. This part is the .../*target* part of the installation.

- Many, Specialized Target Systems

    This is a question of philosophy. Basically, it depends on whether the developer is intended to keep control over his own target's configuration or whether this is intended to be kept under central control. Both ways have their merits.

    Generally, in this case, every developer needs to keep his own copy of the directories .../*target/config/<BSP_name>* and .../*target/config/all* while having a linked tree to all other files.

- Standardized Target Systems

    Anyway, if the target systems are intended to have different but standardized configurations, every configuration should have its own .../*target/config/myconfig1* and .../*target/config/myconfig2* versions of the original .../*target/config/pcore603* directory. This may apply for different memory configurations (even though today many BSPs are auto-configured with regard to memory size) and other add-on functionality.

- Different Projects with the Project Tool and WindNavigator

    Project Tool and WindNavigator are great add-ons to the "old" environment that greatly help developers to stay atop of their code. Anyway, these do not replace the decisions to be made above. The tools are made for a monolithic, single target tree.

If you want to use the installation on several machines which only need to be able to use the include files, a READ-ONLY NFS share will do as long as the target servers are started centrally on a single machine with READ-WRITE access to the .../*.wind* directory.

3.1.2 Setting Up the Host

The first point of discussion is where to put the "original source tree". This depends on the host system architecture and on the space on the hard disks. A full installation needs in the order of 150 MBytes per architecture, not per target board type.

Per BSP, add another 2-4 MBytes.

3.1. INSTALLATIONS

UNIX Hosts

For UNIX systems, choice is very varied. Usual choices are in the areas */usr/local* or */opt*. Keep in mind this should be sharable in case of several development hosts. This directory needs to be shared Read/Write in case of the target servers running on different hosts; at least the directory *.../.wind*. This is where the licensing information is stored.

Windows Hosts

Windows hosts normally live with 1 to 2 hard disks. This makes the choice a lot easier. Here, normally everything should be kept on a central host without local copies. This enables central administration as well as safe file access. Make sure the paths are set up correctly though...

Most systems will create an installation on drive *c:*, usually in the directory *tornado*. Below this directory, the usual tree setup is installed.

3.1.3 Installing the BSP

Until now, only the target's architecture support is installed. The final link to the real hardware is still missing. This link is established by installing the BSP.

Tornado 2

There are two basically identical ways to install BSPs. The normal way to get a BSP is on a CDROM. Here, you can simply install the BSP using the usual setup method as described in the manual [WRS99f].

But, every now and then, you may meet a BSP which comes as a *tar*file. How does one install that? Well, see below.

Prior to Tornado 2

Prior to installing BSPs, the environment variables need to be set up correctly. Otherwise, calling *installOption* will fail. The way they need to be set up is described in [WRS99d] for UNIX and [WRS99e] for Windows.

Basically, the BSP installation files are kept in a *tar* format file[1].

As of VxWorks 5.2, and up into Tornado 1.0, the UNIX versions use a script called *installOption* for the installation. Using only *tar* to do the installation will leave you with an installation that basically works but will result in undefined externals when calling make. This happens because *installOption* not only un-tars the archive but also does some other things:

---

[1] But remember — you should not use *tar* to install the BSP unless it is absolutely impossible to use *installOption*! How to do that in these cases is described on page 29.

- checks the environment for valid variables
- checks file dates
- replaces all older files with their respective new versions
- use ar<architecture> to add/replace any libraries delivered with the BSP into a general archive
- uses ranlib<architecture> to update the library's table of contents.

The library is mentioned in general because it is different for the different versions of VxWorks and Tornado. It will be discussed on the page 36 for VxWorks 5.2, page 35 for Tornado 1.0 and page 35 for Tornado 1.01.

Possible Problems using installOption

Note prior to trying this out, this is not necessary under normal circumstances. This is the very last way out that should be tried only after consulting with your tech support team!

There are basically three possible problems using installOption.

- When the PATH is not set correctly, it may fail because tar and other tools are not found.
- When using installOption with tape archive files, the full path to these files must be specified like installOption -f /home/demo/ demoarchive.option. Otherwise, the script will fail with error messages complaining about non-existing directories even though they actually do exist. In UNIX terms, do not use relative paths!
- This script simply does not exist for Windows hosts. In its place, the batch file below may be used. This is only intended as an example; it needs to be adjusted, depending on the specific setup!

```
@echo off
rem #######################################################
rem #       BSP Installation Script V 0.91             #
rem #     Update VxWorks Tornado BSPs to run with      #
rem #    MS Windows using the WinZip Self Extractor    #
rem #######################################################
rem
rem * setup prerequisites
rem
echo Preparations ...
path %PATH%;%WIND_BASE%\host\x86-win32\bin
set GCC_EXEC_PREFIX=%WIND_BASE%\host\x86-win32\lib\gcc-lib\
```

3.1. INSTALLATIONS

```
rem
rem * copy files to final destination
rem
xcopy *.* %WIND_BASE% /s
rem
rem * now use ar and ranlib to update the libraries
rem
cd %WIND_BASE%\target\config\force\lib\objPPC604gnufrc
echo Changed Directory to Object directory.
echo Backing up library...
mkdir backup
copy ..\libPPC604gnufrc.a backup
echo Updating library...
arppc cru %WIND_BASE%\target\config\force\lib\libPPC604gnufrc.a \
  frcFlashIdent.o frcFlashSys.o frcFlashType1.o \
  frcFlashType2.o frcFlashType4.o frcFlashType5.o
ranlibppc %WIND_BASE%\target\config\force\lib\libPPC604gnufrc.a
echo done.
exit
```

This batch file does not check for file dates, though. Make sure this does not create any problems because files are overwritten that should not be!

Additionally, it is hard-coded for the lib placed in *target/config/force* and a *PPC604* architecture target. So, you may need to make some changes to make it fit your application/BSP.

Manual Installation

This is the very last way out. Here, also the warning concerning overwriting newer files applies.

Now, you can simply *untar* the archive in the installation's root directory.

Then, *cd* to the *lib* directory. There you will find the library files, according to the naming convention *lib<architecture>*[2]*<toolchain>*[3]*vx.a* for Tornado 1.0 and later, *lib<architecture><toolchain><type>*[4]*.a* for VxWorks 5.2.

Examples: *libMC68060gnudrv.a, libPPC604gnuvx.a*

For each of the libraries *libXXX.a*, there is a directory with the name *objXXX*. In this directory, you find the additional files which need to be added to the respective library. These files are added using the command *ar<architecture>* cru *../libXXX.a <FILE_LIST>*; the options *cru* meaning create if non-existent, replace and update the table of contents.

Now, you still need to manually rewrite the library's table of contents. This is achieved using *ranlib<architecture> ../libXXX.a*.

---
[2] Processor architectures like *MC68060, PPC604, SPARC*
[3] Toolchains like *gnu* for GNU, *green* for Greenhills and *diab* for Diab Data
[4] *vx* for VxWorks functions, *drv* for drivers

```
/tornado2/target/lib $ll
total 56470
-rw-r--r--    1 book      support     4560010 Oct 19  1999 libPPC603gnuvx.a
-rw-r--r--    1 book      support     4559140 Oct 19  1999 libPPC604gnuvx.a
drwxr-xr-x    2 book      support        3584 Oct 19  1999 objPPC603gnuvx
drwxr-xr-x    2 book      support        3584 Oct 19  1999 objPPC604gnuvx
/tornado2/target/lib $arppc tvf libPPC604gnuvx.a
rw-r-----  105/100     1989 Apr 22 09:09 1999 bALib.o
rw-r-----  105/100    13952 Apr 22 09:09 1999 dsmLib.o
[...]
rw-r-----    0/1       9336 Apr 22 10:12 1999 rBuffLib.o
rw-r-----    0/1       6856 Apr 22 09:28 1999 evtLogLib.o
/tornado2/target/lib $arppc x libPPC604gnuvx.a evtLogLib.o
/tornado2/target/lib $ll *o
-rw-r-----    1 book      support        6856 Dec 18 14:53 evtLogLib.o
/tornado2/target/lib $ll objPPC604gnuvx/
total 2708
[...]
-rw-r--r--    1 book      support        6856 Oct 19  1999 evtLogLib.o
[...]
-rw-r--r--    1 book      support        4772 Oct 19  1999 z8530Sio.o
/tornado2/target/lib $
```

Figure 3.1: Library Update Example

As of Tornado 1.01, there is a little addition to this process. Wind River Systems have reworked the BSP Porting Kit which helps developers writing BSPs and gives guidelines for setting up BSPs. Until now, the BSP files could simply be added to the VxWorks source tree where they fit in. If you work with many BSPs from different vendors or even home-brew style ones which may not be written very cleanly and so may accidentally overwrite another BSP's driver, you see that this may create a problem.

There are several ways around this. One is – as Wind River Systems decided to do – to simply disallow writing non-Wind River Systems - files to the tree on any location other than the *target/config* directory. This helps to keep the source tree clean from this type of dirt.

It creates a problem for delivered source code, though. Where to put it? Again, there are basically two ways to get around this in a clean fashion.

- Create an additional subdirectory below *.../target/config* to store the common files in a similar tree using the vendor's name plus *lib*, *h* and *src*.

- Create the sub-hierarchy below the *.../target/config/pcore603* directory.

- Simply add all files in their respective form to the *target/config/pcore603* directory. This is certainly the least-best choice.

3.2 What is Where – The Directory Structure

Both ways have their merits. Decide for yourself which one you want to use or look around for what your vendor chose!

Anyway, you need to make sure all drivers added to these places are added to their respective libraries as well. The description from page 29 applies here as well.

3.2 What is Where – The Directory Structure

So, now we have installed both the operating system and the BSP. Now, we only have the choices whether to start with the original kernel or whether we want to make some changes. For several changes, we need to know more about the directory structure.

The directory structure of VxWorks with the top level defined by *$(WIND_BASE)* spreads over three major parts and two additions, *host*, *share*, *docs*, *.wind* and *target*.

3.2.1 *docs* **directory**

This directory has been introduced as of Tornado 2, replacing the directory *man* described below.

docs contains the complete online documentation delivered with Tornado plus the BSP documentation.

3.2.2 *host* **directory**

This directory contains all host-dependent code and files. The most interesting directory is *.../host/$(WIND_HOST_TYPE)/bin*. It contains all binaries you need for developing your code. This directory should be in your PATH; for UNIX it should be in your PATH in the first place as the Makefiles need GNU Make instead of the standard make as delivered with the operating system. If you get errors when compiling, complaining about commands in the Makefiles, this is the reason.

One thing to be aware of: when SETUP is run by root, *execution* permissions for **other** users may be set incorrectly. This typically ends up in *cpp* complaining about 'unknown option -lang-c89' or other error messages from *as* instead of *as<architecture>*.

Now, you need to check *$(GCC_EXEC_PREFIX)/.../cpp* for accessibility and also *$(WIND_BASE)/host/$(HOST_TYPE)/<processorfamily>*[5]*-wrs-vxworks/bin/as* permissions! Probably, you'll find a problem here.

This directory may be shared in read-only mode.

3.2.3 *setup* **directory**

This directory contains (at least in the Tornado Prototyper version!) the installation CD contents.

---
[5] e.g. *m68k* or *sparc* or *ppc*

3.2.4 *share* directory

This directory contains host-independent files, including TCL code. If you want to make any changes and additions, this is the place to look at. Keep in mind that, no matter what changes you make, the changes will be lost when updating to a new version and, additionally, there is no direct backup. If your changes stop the Tornado environment from working, the only way back if you did not create a backup beforehand will be a reinstall!

This directory may be shared in read-only mode.

3.2.5 *target* directory

This is where the "real thing" happens. Here, all code for your target system is kept, including the include files etc. The main subdirectories will be discussed on the following pages. Your board support package is installed into this subtree. See figure 3.2, page 33, for a graphical depiction of the main directories.

h – The include Files

This subdirectory contains all target-specific header files and much more. The standard C include files are stored here as well as the UNIX-like header files. So, this directory needs to be in the compiler's include-path. It will not be there automatically!

Additionally, the system's specific *Makefile* parts are stored here in subdirectory *.../target/h/make*. The most interesting file in the future will be *rules.bsp*. Here, you can check what is done for which make target and, if necessary, add your own targets.

config – The BSP configuration Directory

Some things to say up front. If you are using the IDE to configure you target, do not touch *config.h* or *configAll.h*! Everything said below does apply for configuration using these two files, and then using *make* on the shell to build your targetg system. This is the case whenever you did some real low-level changes. The comfortable way to do things, and definitely recommended, is to use the Project tool.

Never even think of mixing the two methods!

That said, this directory contains the most interesting parts of the configuration. Mainly there are two or three important directories.

First, the generic directory *all*. This directory contains generic startup code as well as the generic configuration file *configAll.h*. Here, the modules to be included may be selected.

You should be aware that this directory will be used by all installations. Sharing this *.../target/config* directory will also share the settings as set in *configAll.h*.

The latest definitions by Wind River Systems, when making changes base on the config file, say that you should make adjustments *not* to *configAll.h* but to *config.h*. The reason is clear above. See page 36 below for more info.

3.2. WHAT IS WHERE – THE DIRECTORY STRUCTURE

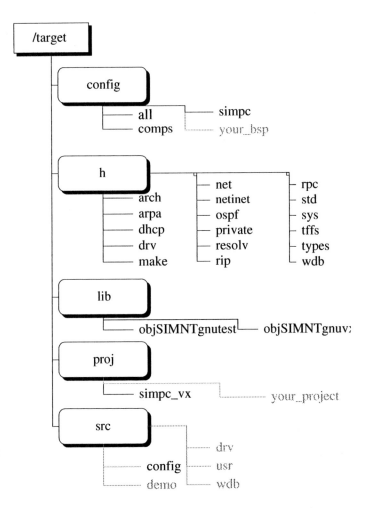

Figure 3.2: *target* subtree of the installation

With Tornado 2, this has all become obsolete anyway except for special adjustments. All other settings should be made using the project tool or the project module in the IDE!

The second, even more interesting, directory is the BSP directory. Here, some BSP specific code is stored as well as the main BSP configuration file, *config.h*. Also, when building the kernel manually, this is the directory in which to execute *make*. For descriptions of the different targets, see page 38. For more information on related files and their contents, just read on!

src – Additional Source Codes

This directory contains Wind River-standard source code subdirectories, drivers etc. It has several subdirectories which contain subdivided code:

- *config*

    This subdirectory has several O/S files which may need to be edited to reflect the system specific configuration, like *usrScsi.c*, *usrNetwork.c*, *usrExtra.c* and *usrLib.c*. Find more information on the different files and their meanings on page 105 in Chapter 7.1.

    Tornado 1   Note, when using the target shell with Tornado 1, *usrLib.c* by default may contain many of the target-executed, shell-built-in commands. However, it is also delivered in object code as part of the system libraries. So, if you want to change these commands' behavior or add functions to this file, you must recompile and then, using *ar<architecture>* and *ranlib<architecture>* update it in the standard library.

- *demo*

    This directory contains some demo code that is definitely worth a look if you have just started using VxWorks or need some additional tools:

    1   This is a simple client/server demo that has two programs talking to each other.

    color   A colored demo for interprocess communication.

    cplusplus   A simple demo for object creation and deletion to show C++.

    dg   A demo for UNIX sending and receiving UDP packets.

3.2. WHAT IS WHERE – THE DIRECTORY STRUCTURE 35

echo Similar to the demo above but using TCP sockets. The application reads data and then echoes it back.

net This directory has some interesting contents. It contains scripts that allow instrumentation of the network stack for WindView so you can see the different events there. See the short but complete *readme* for more information.

start This is the demo code used in the Getting Started manual.

wind This is a test program for the kernel. See the source code for more information.

- *drv*

  Here you will find source delivered drivers for purposes like VME, mem(ory) or intctl (interrupt controllers). If you are looking for a specific driver, look here first! If you cannot find the necessary driver, ask your board vendor and Wind River for availability.

- *usr*

  As of Tornado 2, this directory contains the file *usrLib.c* as pointed out above on page 34 for Tornado 1.

  Also, *memDrv.c* is a simple driver that allows access to memory through a pseudo device. This will be of interest when writing device drivers to get a first feeling of how things work.

  If you need a file system, *ramDrv.c* is source for a RAM drive. There is a normal ramdrive included anyway, so there is only limited use for the source code...

- *wdb*

  This directory contains UDP libraries for WDB.

lib – Global Libraries

Here, the global libraries are stored. As described on page 29 in the chapter on Manual BSP Installation, in the adjacent subdirectories, added drivers for e.g. WindView etc. are stored which then using the *installOption* are also added to the system libraries.

man – Documentation (up to Tornado 1 only)

This subtree contains the documentation in UNIX *man* format. This format basically shows function, library and program descriptions as printed in the Reference Manual, [WRS991].

Text formatted *man* pages were reintroduced in Tornado 2.2.

unsupported – **Additional Code And Tools**

This subsection contains accessories which are not supported by Wind River but which are nice to have and to use. Additionally, here we can find unsupported ports of Vx-Works for other boards, *bootp* implementations etc. This area certainly contains useful code, so simply have a look!

This directory has been removed in Tornado 2.

3.2.6 But There is Still More - *.wind*

OK, let us start with some UNIX background – in UNIX, files which start with "." are hidden in normal directory displays.

And that is also the case for this directory. Here, the license managers, both ELAN and FlexLM (Tornado version dependent) store their license information. Because it also writes to this directory, the directory has to be *writable* for all hosts using the installation and acting as hosts for target servers. The directory also should be pointed to by the environment variable **LM_LICENSE_PATH** if it is not in the default place or if problems occur. This is something to verify!

3.2.7 The Old Times — Before Tornado

Before Tornado, this separation did not exist. All directories were on the same level. Making the differences between read-only and read-write directories was a lot harder. Anyway, if you need more information on this, contact the author directly.

3.3 Configuration Basics

This part describes some basic information on building the kernel and how changes to the setup can be made.

3.3.1 Configuration Tool & Project Workspace

Before discussing the specifics, some remarks on how the configuration tools work in general.

Tornado 1

The Configuration Tool of Tornado 1 adds a line to the end of *config.h* which `#includes` an additional *configdb.h* file. This file, first of all, `#undefines` nearly all options which may be selected in *configAll.h*. Then, depending on the user's choice, it `#defines` the options the user selected.

So, in a general fashion, this file obliterates *configAll.h*. But, there are some principal things one should keep in mind.

3.3. CONFIGURATION BASICS

First of all, some settings in *configAll.h* still persist. These are settings like *smNetwork* settings.

Additionally, some settings in *config.h* may depend on choices in *configAll.h*. These may still be set to the original settings, no matter what settings the user may have selected in the configuration tool. The configuration is included *at the end*, something to remember!

Finally, there are BSP specific settings (e.g. flash libraries, additional network protocols and others). These are not available in the configuration tool either. So, whatever you do, make sure you read the BSP documentation first.

Tornado 2

The configuration tool only survived one version, and was replaced by the project tool. The project tool introduces a new level of awareness of the tools, also greatly adding to configurability.

However, the project tool keeps the *config.h* configurations alive while obsoleting the *configAll.h* configurations. There are in fact now two *configAll.h* files that are used, depending on how you choose to build your system:

- When using the IDE to build,

  the system will use a bare-bones edition of *configAll.h* that is copied to your project directory. The settings are made through the additionally included file *prjParams.h*, that is included by *config.h*. This file is created and configured through the IDE. Do not edit it! The warning mentioned before on page 32 applies!

  Also note, that changes to Makefile and header files will only make it into the project if the project is re-created! Changes to C files will be carried over, though.

- When building from the command line using *make*,

  the system will continue to use the "old" *configAll.h* file that may be edited to meet your needs.

Again, do not mix both methods!

3.3.2 Rebuilding the Kernel

To rebuild the kernel, there are several possibilities. The simple way is to open the Build menu and select "build Kernel". This will use the current project's configuration and create the kernel according to it.

When would you do that? Tornado comes with a fairly general kernel configuration that is well suited for most needs. But, as you walk through your development process, you may find that some features are necessary but not included, yet. Another reason could be that you need to include additional drivers that are not part of the default configuration or support additional devices such as PMC cards or other extension cards. Finally, at the end of your development cycle, you may find that either the kernel is too big or you just do not need certain features. For instance to speed up unpacking, remove unneeded or undesired features. For development, a target shell connected to the serial port is a nice thing, but do you want your customer to be able to use it?

Anyway, something to consider is that you may still need some additional features to debug a possible crash in service. But that is something to discuss later in the 6th chapter.

Another way is to open a shell and run *make*. As described in appendix B, there are several possible targets to run *make* on. The safe choice is to execute *make clean release*. This first removes all intermediate files, object modules and resulting modules and then creates a standard set of target files, *vxWorks*, *vxWorks.sym*, *vxWorks.st* and *bootrom*. More, and different kernel versions are discussed below, in section 3.4 plus the different tasks they serve.

3.4 Different Goals, different Kernels

The standard *Makefile* as delivered offers quite a bunch of possible targets to build. These targets are discussed in this chapter.

There are two different basic modules for the different VxWorks builds, the *bootrom* and the kernel, called *vxWorks**. The *bootrom* serves the initial board startup plus initialization of the boot parameters as shown in chapter 4.1.1. This is basically a stripped-down version of the normal kernel.

The *vxWorks.** variants, with the exception of *vxWorks.sym* are the different versions of the kernel.

All files ending with **.hex* are SRECORD versions of the respective versions without this postfix.

You can also find detailed descriptions of all targets supported by *make* in the file *.../target/h/make/rules.bsp*.

3.4.1 Bootrom

The bootrom represents the initial step of the boot process. If you need to set up parameters prior to starting your target, this is the place to do so. Actually, it should better be called "boot loader", beacuse that is what it does. the name stems from the old days, when you would really burn EPROMS with the bootrom code in them.

The file is in fact a miniature version of VxWorks, with the kernel and a minimum of drivers in it.

3.4. DIFFERENT GOALS, DIFFERENT KERNELS

bootrom

The make target *bootrom* creates a compressed version of the bootrom, which starts in ROM, copies the data to RAM, unpacks there and then starts the real bootrom code. So, this is the smallest variant of the bootrom. If you have a problem with the packing algorithm or the time it takes to unpack, though, this may lead to further problems.

bootrom_uncmp

For this case, the uncompressed bootrom exists. It copies its own code to RAM and starts it there. The advantage is that the bootrom does not need to unpack and so starts faster. The disadvantage is that it consumes more space in the physical bootrom. Again, this is a tradeoff, depending on what you need.

3.4.2 Kernel

Of course, there are more variants of the kernel because this is the base of the target system. All kernels have to assume that there is no other program before that might initialize any chip, so that they have to do all the setup themselves.

That said, let us have a look at them...

vxWorks

This is the standard version of the VxWorks system. This kernel starts wdb, and then remains more or less silently on the target system. Unless specified differently, there is no target shell available. If the target shell is enabled, though, this kernel will also load its symbol table from *vxWorks.sym*.

vxWorks.st

This is the standalone (hence .*st*) version of the kernel. It still needs the bootrom, but then starts without initializing the networking or executing any network accesses.

Both target shell and symbol table are compiled-in. There is no networking possible; to start it, you need to set the parameters correctly using **bootChange()** and then execute **usrNetInit()**.

Another way to have networking in the standalone kernels is to edit the file .../target/h/make/rules.bsp, look for -DSTANDALONE and for each one, you also need to add -DSTANDALONE_NET. If this is set, the bootparameters will be read, interpreted and obeyed to set the different networking parameters. They need to be valid for this!

vxWorks_rom

This version of the kernel does not include a symbol table, so commands from the shell or downloads from whatever place are impossible. Additionally, no networking

```
vxWorks.st_rom.uncmp : depend.$(BSP_NAME) usrConfig_st.o \
                       dataSegPad.o bootInit_uncmp.o \
                       romInit.o sysALib.o sysLib.o \
                       $(LDDEPS) $(LIBS) $(BOOT_EXTRA)
    - @ $(RM) symTbl.c
    - @ $(RM) symTbl.o
    - @ $(RM) version.o
    - @ $(RM) ctdt.c ctdt.o
    $(CC) -c $(CFLAGS) -o version.o $(CONFIG_ALL)/version.c
    $(LD) -o tmp.1 -e $(SYS_ENTRY) $(LD_PARTIAL_FLAGS) \
          dataSegPad.o $(MACH_DEP) usrConfig_st.o $(LIBS)
    $(MKSYMTBL) tmp.1 >symTbl.c
    $(COMPILE_SYMTBL) symTbl.c
    $(NM) tmp.1 | $(MUNCH) >ctdt.c
    $(MAKE) CC_COMPILER="-traditional" ctdt.o
    $(LD) $(LDFLAGS) -e $(ROM_ENTRY) $(LD_LOW_FLAGS) \
          -o $@ romInit.o bootInit_uncmp.o version.o tmp.1 \
          symTbl.o ctdt.o $ (BOOT_EXTRA) $(LIBS)
    $(ROMSIZEPROG) -b $(ROM_SIZE) $@
    $(LDOUT_CONV) $@

vxWorks.st_rom.uncmp.hex : depend.$(BSP_NAME) vxWorks.st_rom.uncmp $(IMI)
    - @ $(RM) $@
    $(BINHEX) $(HEX_FLAGS) \
              $(SECT_SPEC)vxWorks.st_rom.uncmp$(TXT_OFFSET) \
              $(IMI_SPEC)$(IMI)$(IMI_OFFSET) > $@$(MAP_EXT)
    -@ $(MV_BIN)
```

Figure 3.3: Addition to *rules.bsp* to allow uncompressed, rommable kernel

is initialized. The way described above does work, but, again, no local symbol table is available!

vxWorks.st_rom

This a version of the kernel which does not need the *bootrom*. The kernel starts from ROM and copies and uncompresses itself to RAM when started. It includes the symbol table, so the system can be totally standalone. For networking, the above rule applies.

vxWorks.st_rom.uncmp

This *make* target does not exist. But, as some people may find this helpful, here is what would need to be in *.../target/h/make/rules.bsp*.

Everything that is true for *vxWorks.st_rom* is true here also, but no compression is used. That is the difference.

Chapter 4

Booting the Target

The very first process when starting a new target is to boot it. In VxWorks, in most cases, the original boot software as delivered with the board itself is replaced with bootroms delivered with the BSP.

On other boards, the VxWorks bootrom is added to the original bootrom. There are other ways of booting VxWorks which will be discussed later in this chapter.

For board specific information, there are several sources of information, *target.nr* containing the information in *troff* format, *target.txt* in text mode and, of course the Release Notes that are part of the documentation.

Simulator The Simulator is a special case here. Of course, it only simulates a target and so is not in need of a first bootrom. The O/S running below has booted anyway...! So, the bootrom step can be ignored here but will be necessary for a future real target.

4.1 The bootrom

After inserting the physical bootroms and powering up the board, you find yourself in the so-called bootrom; basically this is a minimal version of the first-level kernel functionality with the simplest drivers. After entering the boot parameters, a first attempt to boot the board can be made.

4.1.1 The Parameters

There are a lot of possible parameters to adjust in the bootrom. Some of them affect the boot process, others direct additional functionality.

There is one very important command to gather more information, `help`. This command also delivers information on compiled-in options.

Boot Device

Possible choices are shown at the end of the output of the `help` command as visible in figure 4.1. The parameters and their function are presented in table 4.1 below.

Device Name	Device
frcDec	FORCE version of DEC 21140 Ethernet driver
bp	Old, VxWorks 5.0 backplane network driver (for compatibility only[1])
sm	Shared Memory Network, see chapter 4.1.5, page 57

Table 4.1: Standard Boot Devices for PowerCore-6604

Processor Number

The processor number. This number is used for several different purposes depending on your target:

- Bus slave address (both VME and cPCI)

  In VxWorks, the slave address is normally computed using the Processor Number. The usual equation is:

  $slaveAdrs = baseAdrs + ProcessorNumber * WindowSize$

  The computation valid for you can be found in *config.h*. Look for **sysProcNumGet()** there! Doing this for the simulator yields — nothing. Of course, normally, the simulator runs on a standard PC, not in a backplane bus system!

  Some older BSPs may open the slave window for the board with processor number 0 only. Check *syslib.c* to find out whether or not this is the case for you if you have problems here. The reason for this behavior is the way the Shared Memory Network works — you only need access to the shared memory master's slave memory. Or, if you are using a memory board for the Shared Memory Network, no slave window at all.

- Shared Memory Network Master Function

  In the standard setup, the board with Processor Number 0 is defined as the master of the Shared Memory Network. This board is the communications controller for the shared memory network.

4.1. THE BOOTROM

```
[VxWorks Boot]: help

?                            - print this list
@                            - boot (load and go)
p                            - print boot params
c                            - change boot params
l                            - load boot file
g adrs                       - go to adrs
d adrs[,n]                   - display memory
m adrs                       - modify memory
f adrs, nbytes, value        - fill memory
t adrs, adrs, nbytes         - copy memory
e                            - print fatal exception
n netif                      - print network interface device address
$dev(0,procnum)host:/file h=# e=# b=# g=# u=usr [pw=passwd] f=#
                              tn=targetname s=script o=other
Boot flags:
  0x02   - load local system symbols
  0x04   - don't autoboot
  0x08   - quick autoboot (no countdown)
  0x20   - disable login security
  0x40   - use bootp to get boot parameters
  0x80   - use tftp to get boot image
  0x100  - use proxy arp

available boot devices: frcDec bp sm
[VxWorks Boot]:
```

Figure 4.1: Example output for help command at the bootprompt

The sm parameter may be postfixed with an address for the Shared Memory Network Anchor, e.g. sm=0x80004100. This address is specified as seen from the local CPU. Use a kernel compiled with the same configuration as the bootrom plus a **sysBusToLocalAdrs(AnchorBusAdrs)** call to determine where to look for it.

Host Name

This is the hostname VxWorks will use for the host system. As VxWorks does not know about DNS in its default configuration, it uses a static method for mapping hostnames to IP addresses. For this the function **hostAdd()** is used internally. If you want to use additional host names instead of IP addresses, you will have to use this function to create the appropriate table entries.

This behavior has changed partially with the introduction of SENS. VxWorks now knows about DNS, but only if it is enabled! Do not take it for granted, though! And, keep in mind to set the correct parameter settings for your DNS server in *configAll.h*, looking for DNS!

44   CHAPTER 4. BOOTING THE TARGET

Boot File

This is the kernel file to be loaded. Depending on the way this kernel is built it determines the features available as well as some basic behaviors of the system.

Inet on Ethernet

This line contains the IP address and net mask of the target system. If the net mask is not specified, the IP stack will determine it and set it accordingly.

Inet on Backplane

This line contains the IP address of the target system on the backplane, if the Shared Memory Network is being used. This may also be used for FORCE's BusNet protocol software.

Normally, the transfer of the board's boot file from the host is handled through the gateway.

If this field contains an IP address but the boot device is not *sm*, the shared memory network driver will be initialized *in addition to the normal Ethernet interface*. The IP stack will be configured to act as a router. Otherwise, the only network interface initialized will be this interface. You should also know that this configuration makes the target send RIP packets [2], telling other devices that this device is a router. This may lead to network issues such as addresses suddenly not being accessible any more etc. So, watch out here![3]

Host Inet

This is the host's IP address. VxWorks will map this IP address to the host name as specified above. So, to avoid confusion, better make sure you use the standard name you use in your network!

Gateway Inet

VxWorks doesn't know how to route by default. So, if your boot host is on a different network than the target system, you have to tell it how to get there! This is the gateway host's IP address. Additionally, this will have to be used in the case of the Shared Memory Network to specify the routing information.

If there is no gateway defined, but `Host Inet` and `Inet on XXX` — according to selected boot device — are on different networks, you will simply see nothing happen when trying to boot. There will not even be packets on the network! Problem here is that you will have no indication at all what is wrong, just nothing happening.

---

[2] Router Information Protocol packets
[3] Note, that older VxWorks versions malfunctioned and did not or only under certain, seldom circumstances send these packets. In this case, for once a beneficial bug, preventing network problems!

4.1. THE BOOTROM

The only thing to do is to leave it alone and return later to recheck the parameter set or ask someone else to compare.

User

This is the user name to use to access files on the host.

This is a common cause for problems. If your target system has problems downloading the kernel, make sure it can actually access the file! To be sure, *rsh* to your host and try to *cp* the file. Use Copy-Paste to test the filename, including the complete path!

FTP Password

If this is supplied, VxWorks will use *ftp* to access host files. Otherwise, it will use *rsh* plus the program *cat* to download any file.

FTP permissions are a possible source of problems, too. See chapter 4.3, page 60.

Flags

The flags determine additional behavior, some of them concerning the bootrom's behavior, others the kernel's behavior once it is downloaded. The flags and their meanings are also displayed when executing `help` at the bootprompt, see figure 4.1 above.

Some with interesting behavior or features merit being mentioned below.

- 0x02

    Local symbols can be of help if you need to debug unusual, internal behavior. Many libraries have local symbols which can be set to a non-zero value to get more information. This is the way to get access to them.

- 0x04, 0x08

    Autoboot options allow to change the default behavior of the boot by either stopping the autoboot functionality of the bootrom or by disabling the countdown completely. Beware, though, that this also prohibits your access to the bootparameters if the kernel does not come up correctly...

- 0x80

    TFTP to get the kernel is a nice function. Just remember to also enable this for the kernel itself, otherwise the kernel will be downloaded using TFTP, but the symbol table will be retrieved using FTP. Just to point out a possible problem. TFTP is explained on page 47 below.

Target Name

This name will be used for the target. The name being used towards the network is not affected by this, it is only used internally! However, the cleanest solution is to have all those names identical to avoid confusion.

Startup

This script is downloaded from the host after booting the kernel and then executed. This will only work if the target-resident shell and symbol table are included. Otherwise, this field is ignored.

Options

Here, additional options can be passed to the kernel.

An example usage for this field is the initialization of the network even though the target system is booted from a non-network device like SCSI or has two Ethernet interfaces. This depends on your system setup. Be sure to check the corresponding files like *usrNetwork.c* etc. if you are interested in using this feature.

You may also use it for your own purposes.

4.1.2 Bootrom Development – When and How

Bootrom Development is necessary only in cases where you need to include boot off on-supported devices or additional devices like PMC or other extension cards. Another reason may be the need for a specific behavior that is not part of the standard bootrom. As an example, we will add SCSI boot to the bootrom below.

There are several possibilities of how to get the bootrom software into the target system. For final production versions, PROMs of one or another type are convenient. For development purposes, burning new PROMs for every new test run is not as convenient. There are different ways of doing this so we will look at both ways in the following examples.

PROM boot

Today, a PROM normally is a flash memory chip. This shows the convenience of being able to reprogram the chip from a running system.

The downside should not go unmentioned. Of course, if something goes wrong while reprogramming the bootrom, your system will be unable to boot any more. So, never go for these kind of tests without a backup bootprom somewhere!

A description where to find the correct bootrom and how to replace it is part of the BSP documentation. Some boards have soldered boot PROMS, others have sockets. See the documentation for more information!

4.1. THE BOOTROM

Bootrom Download via the Network

This is most convenient for development purposes. Build a new bootrom file, download and test it. Continue development and download it again ...

But, it is not possible for every architecture and BSP. Contact your BSP's manufacturer whether this mode is possible or not. The reason is that both the creation of a bootrom that can be downloaded and creation of a firmware that supports downloading and starting code are no simple tasks. Anyway, for the next few lines of text, let us assume you can do it.

How does it work?

The most common way is to boot via TFTP.

TFTP stands for Trivial File Transfer Protocol. It is a simpler implementation of FTP with less features but ideally suited for network boot scenarios. You do not need a user name and only few permissions, so it also offers fairly safe ways of getting to your kernel (however applies to everyone!).

As there are only very few TFTP servers for Windows, we will discuss the way this works for UNIX, specifically in this example, Solaris 2.x hosts.

First, the server needs to be able to deliver the TFTP service. So, check the file */etc/inetd.conf* that the TFTP service is enabled. For an example entry, see figure 4.2.

```
#
# Tftp service is provided primarily for booting.  Most sites run this
# only on machines acting as "boot servers."
#
tftp     dgram    udp     wait    root    /usr/sbin/in.tftpd \
         in.tftpd -s /tftpboot
```

Figure 4.2: Excerpt from */etc/inetd.conf*

Then, create the directory */tftpboot*. This directory must have the permissions 777, allowing all kinds of access to everyone. In it, add a link to itself named *tftpboot*[4].

Now, use *ps* to find the process number for *inetd* and then use *kill -HUP <process number>* to restart *inetd*.

Enter the Ethernet address and host name of your target in */etc/ethers*; if this file does not exist, create it. Make sure this file also maps the host name to a valid IP address as defined in */etc/hosts* or DNS. An example entry for */etc/ethers* can be found in figure 4.3 on page 47.

```
00:80:42:a:13:d9           ios2      # Example Host Entry
```

Figure 4.3: Sample entry from */etc/ethers*

---
[4]This is due to the fact that early versions of the OpenBoot bootprom had a bug which did not remove the /tftpboot from the requested file and is only valid for SPARC based boards.

Now, the setup is finished.

RARP and TFTP – Network boot without the VxWorks BootROM inserted

This describes the way most simple booters try to get files from the network.

If your target tries to boot from the network, it normally sends a RARP (Remote Address Resolution Protocol) message.

The host receives this message, checks its /etc/ethers for the Ethernet address and, if successful, and the target exists in /etc/hosts or DNS, answers with the target's IP address. Now, the target requests the file to download via TFTP, normally from the host which responded with the IP address. The way the filename is constructed depends on the target's firmware.

As MS Windows doesn't provide for this, to be able to download the bootrom, you need to check that your target system doesn't depend on RARP. Some booters today provide a means to start TFTP without the RARP cycle up front by allowing the user to directly enter IP addresses.

4.1.3 Network Boot

Now we have got the bootrom on our target, we want to finally download the kernel. To get it from the network, there is basically only the way to use the board's network interface or the Shared Memory network, which is described in chapter 4.1.5, page 57.

This is the most convenient way while developing, because this way, in a new iteration while still making changes to the kernel, you simply reboot the target system. Every other way like booting from SCSI or flash means that you need to re-program or re-copy the image to its final location.

However, for deployment, you may want to choose SCSI devices or flash devices to store the kernel.

4.1.4 SCSI Boot

Another likely boot method for standalone production target systems is boot from SCSI devices. To be able to do this, a few changes need to be made and some adaptations have to be made as well.

Enabling SCSI

First, you need to build a bootrom which has the ability to boot from SCSI. To verify this, type `help` at the bootprompt. At the end of the output, you will find a list of possible boot devices. The standard bootrom as delivered does *not* have SCSI boot enabled, see figure 4.1 on page 43. So, look for "scsi" in the list of possible boot devices.

Nothing there?

4.1. THE BOOTROM

Partition (SCSI ID, LUN)	Partition Number	Format	Type
2,0	0	DOS	Harddisk
2,0	1	RT-11	Harddisk
2,0	2	RT-11	Harddisk

Table 4.2: *usrScsi.c* SCSI Default Setup

OK, let's get started.

Preparing the Bootrom

First of all, you need to setup .../*target/config/<bspdirectory>/config.h* to enable SCSI. This is fairly simple: search for SCSI, and you will find a section which holds all necessary defines but is disabled using #if FALSE. Setting this to #if TRUE will enable SCSI. Additionally, remember you want to boot from SCSI, so you need to enable the #define SCSI_BOOT as well. If you need your own SCSI setup as defined in the file .../*target/src/config/usrScsi.c* to be executed, you will also need to #define SYS_SCSI_CONFIG, and then edit .../*target/src/config/usrScsi.c*. This is described below.

You should *not* #define SCSI_AUTO_CONFIG because that will just generally search for and define SCSI devices connected to the SCSI bus. This may be useful for debug operations to check that SCSI works, but is not a good idea for production systems with a fixed set of SCSI devices connected.

Now, rebuild kernel plus bootrom. The safest way to achieve this is to go to the BSP directory and execute *make clean release*.

Preparing the Kernel

After setting up the bootrom, the kernel setup needs to be finalized. To do so, you need to edit the file *target/src/config/usrScsi.c* or, as recommended there, create your own **sysScsiConfig()** function in *sysLib.c*. Why? Because this directory applies to *all* BSPs!

Let us follow the default configuration defined there and pretend that we may edit the file to keep life simple. The example configuration used in this file is shown in table 4.1.4.

You now need to do the following: to enable your own code to be used as shown below in figure 4.4, you need to change the #if FALSE to #if TRUE. Also, you should disable the scsiDebug = TRUE and scsiIntsDebug = TRUE setup by setting them to FALSE. Otherwise, you will see a lot of messages which may prove helpful when debugging, but for the beginning, they only disturb. If you encounter problems, re-enable scsiDebug first. Otherwise, you will be swamped with masses of messages which probably will not yield the information you need.

You also need to enable using the function by `#define USR_SCSI_CONFIG` in *config.h*.

After the definitions for the Hard Drives, there are definitions for tape and floppy. Insert `#endif` and `#if FALSE` before them to keep them unused.

This setup needs to be changed to reflect your actual setup. For our example, let us assume the configuration as shown below: To make life simple, we use a SCSI disk, jumpered to SCSI ID 3, LUN 0^5, create a single partition on it, to be formatted using the *dosFs*. See the code in figure 4.5.

Additionally, the device name to boot from is hard-coded into the example as delivered. So, this has to be changed as well. Search for "/sd0/" and replace it with the name you choose for your hard disk. In this example, we will use "scsi3:/" for SCSI device with SCSI ID 3. You will also need to search and replace "/sd0/" in *.../target/config/all/bootConfig.c* to have the `help` command reflect the correct setup. If you do not need this, you may skip this step. For the purpose of consistency in the overall system, skipping it is definitely not recommended.

So, now you need to set up the boot disk.

Preparing the SCSI Bootdisk

Now you first need to create a device in the operating system, then create a file system on it, format it and finally, create directories on it and save the kernel to it. Then, we can boot from the SCSI disk. So, let us start by telling the O/S about the hard disk.

Remark: All examples below show the output directly below the command. If you are using windsh together with the target agent, you will probably see this output on the terminal connected to the console!

First of all, let us start from the beginning to be sure everything is set up as expected:

```
-> scsiAutoConfig
value = 0 = 0x0
-> scsiShow
ID LUN VendorID     ProductID         Rev. Type  Blocks   BlkSize pScsiPhysDev
-- --- --------     ---------------   ---- ----  -------- ------- ------------
 3  0  SEAGATE      ST32151N          0154    0  4197405     512  0x00ffe6c8
value = 0 = 0x0
```

Now, we create a block device and then a DOS file system on the hard disk. The pointer to the SCSI controller (`pSysScsiCtrl`) is a global variable which is initialized by the BSP. Obviously, this may create a problem if you have two SCSI controllers available...

```
-> pSbd30=scsiBlkDevCreate(scsiPhysDevIdGet(pSysScsiCtrl,3,0),0,0)
new symbol "pSbd30" added to symbol table.
pSbd30 = 0xffd310: value = 16765736 = 0xffd328 = pSbd30 + 0x18
```

---

[5] Logical Unit Numbers are not in use today any more. Use the default value 0 wherever you need it.

4.1. THE BOOTROM

```
/*
 * HARD DRIVE CONFIGURATION
 *
 * In order to configure a hard disk and initialize both dosFs and rt11Fs
 * file systems, the following initialization code will serve as an
 * example.
 */

/* configure a SCSI hard disk at busId = 2, LUN = 0 */
if ((pSpd20 = scsiPhysDevCreate (pSysScsiCtrl, 2, 0, 0, NONE, 0, 0, 0))
    == (SCSI_PHYS_DEV *) NULL)
    {
    printErr ("usrScsiConfig: scsiPhysDevCreate failed.\n",
              0, 0, 0, 0, 0, 0);
    }
else
    {
    /* create block devices */

    if (((pSbd0 = scsiBlkDevCreate (pSpd20, 0x10000, 0)) == NULL)       ||
        ((pSbd1 = scsiBlkDevCreate (pSpd20, 0x10000, 0x10000)) == NULL) ||
        ((pSbd2 = scsiBlkDevCreate (pSpd20, 0, 0x20000)) == NULL))
        {
        return (ERROR);
        }

    if ((dosFsDevInit ("/sd0/", pSbd0, NULL) == NULL) )
        {
        return (ERROR);
        }
#ifdef INCLUDE_RT11FS
        if ((rt11FsDevInit ("/sd1/", pSbd1, 0, 256, TRUE) == NULL) ||
            (rt11FsDevInit ("/sd2/", pSbd2, 0, 256, TRUE) == NULL))
            {
            return (ERROR);
            }
#endif
    }
```

Figure 4.4: Excerpt from *usrScsi.c*: Default SCSI Configuration

```
/*
 * HARD DRIVE CONFIGURATION
 *
 * This is a sample on how to setup a hard disk with a single partition
 * using the package dosFs
 *
 */

/* configure a SCSI hard disk at busId = 3, LUN = 0 */

if ((pSpd30 = scsiPhysDevCreate (pSysScsiCtrl, 3, 0, 0, NONE, 0, 0, 0))
    == (SCSI_PHYS_DEV *) NULL)
    {
    printErr ("usrScsiConfig: scsiPhysDevCreate failed.\n",
                  0, 0, 0, 0, 0, 0);
    }
else
    {
    /* create block devices */

    if ((pSbd30 = scsiBlkDevCreate (pSpd30, 0, 0)) == NULL)
        {
        return (ERROR);
        }

    if ((dosFsDevInit ("scsi3:/", pSbd30, NULL) == NULL) )
        {
        return (ERROR);
        }
    }
```

Figure 4.5: Excerpt from *usrScsi.c*: Our example SCSI Configuration

4.1. THE BOOTROM 53

```
-> dosFsMkfs("scsi3:/",pSbd30)
value = 16765504 = 0xffd240
-> iosDevShow
drv name
  0 /null
  1 /tyCo/0
  5 host:
  6 /pty/rlogin.S
  7 /pty/rlogin.M
  6 /pty/telnet.S
  7 /pty/telnet.M
  3 scsi3:/
value = 25 = 0x19
->
```

If **dosfsMkfs()** fails (indicated by returning NULL), the command **scsiFormatUnit()** has to be used to initialize the device before creating the filesystem.

Remark: **iosDevShow()** *allows to list the devices that are known to the I/O system. If you add SCSI devices or others, they have to show up in this table; if they do not, something is seriously wrong. So, this is a way to verify that the* **dosFsMkfs()** *call definitely was successful. However, it does* **not** *mean that the device is functioning properly; it just means that it can return the correct information.*

Now, let us enter the device and create a directory on it to check that everything is ok:

```
-> cd "scsi3:/"
value = 0 = 0x0
-> ll
value = 0 = 0x0
-> mkdir "vxWorks"
value = 0 = 0x0
-> ll
  size        date      time      name
--------    ------    ------    --------
   512    JAN-01-1980 00:00:00  VXWORKS            <DIR>
value = 0 = 0x0
```

We now need the kernel on the hard disk. So, let us **copy()** it here; we need to add the "host:" at the beginning of the **copy()** command because all of them get executed relatively to the current device root (i.e. after the cd "scsi3:/", relatively to this root directory)! Additionally, cd "scsi3:" will only try a local **cd()**.

You should also remember that **cd()** and **copy()** are C functions which expect strings in quotes as parameters.

```
-> copy "host:/home/chwe/work/pcore/target/config/pcore603/vxWorks",
   "scsi3:/vxWorks/vxWorks"
value = 0 = 0x0
-> copy "host:/home/chwe/work/pcore/target/config/pcore603/vxWorks.sym",
```

```
"scsi3:/vxWorks/vxWorks.sym"
value = 0 = 0x0
-> ll "scsi3:/vxWorks"
  size         date         time        name
--------      ------       ------     --------
   512     JAN-01-1980   00:00:00        .              <DIR>
   512     JAN-01-1980   00:00:00        ..             <DIR>
880639     JAN-01-1980   00:00:00     VXWORKS
115667     JAN-01-1980   00:00:00     VXWORKS.SYM
value = 0 = 0x0
->
```

To find more information on the device, use **dosFsConfigShow()**[6]:

```
-> dosFsConfigShow
device name:                scsi3:/
total number of sectors:    4197405
bytes per sector:           512
media byte:                 0xf0
# of sectors per cluster:   65
# of reserved sectors:      1
# of FAT tables:            2
# of sectors per FAT:       253
max # of root dir entries:  112
# of hidden sectors:        0
removable medium:           false
disk change w/out warning:  not enabled
auto-sync mode:             not enabled
long file names:            not enabled
exportable file system:     not enabled
lowercase-only filenames:   not enabled
volume mode:                O_RDWR (read/write)
available space:            2147724800 bytes
max avail. config space:    2147724800 bytes
value = 0 = 0x0
->
```

Testing the Setup

After all this, we now need to check the set up. First check that the reprogrammed bootrom now knows about SCSI:

```
[VxWorks Boot]: help

  ?                    - print this list
  @                    - boot (load and go)
  p                    - print boot params
  c                    - change boot params
  l                    - load boot file
```

---

[6]Note: sizes may be shown incorrectly if they exceed 4 GB.

4.1. THE BOOTROM

```
g adrs                     - go to adrs
d adrs[,n]                 - display memory
m adrs                     - modify memory
f adrs, nbytes, value      - fill memory
t adrs, adrs, nbytes       - copy memory
e                          - print fatal exception
n netif                    - print network interface device address
$dev(0,procnum)host:/file h=# e=# b=# g=# u=usr [pw=passwd] f=#
                             tn=targetname s=script o=other
boot device: scsi=id,lun              file name: scsi3:/vxWorks
Boot flags:
  0x02  - load local system symbols
  0x04  - don't autoboot
  0x08  - quick autoboot (no countdown)
  0x20  - disable login security
  0x40  - use bootp to get boot parameters
  0x80  - use tftp to get boot image
  0x100 - use proxy arp

available boot devices: frcDc bp sm scsi
[VxWorks Boot]:
```

There it is!
Now, start the boot by first setting up the new parameter set. Note that the kernel used for this demo has the target shell enabled.

```
[VxWorks Boot]: c

'.' = clear field;  '-' = go to previous field;   ^D = quit

boot device            : frcDc scsi=3,0
processor number       : 0
host name              : ios
file name              : /home/chwe/work/PCore/target/config/pcore604/vxWorks
                         scsi3://vxWorks/vxWorks
inet on ethernet (e)   : 192.168.101.32:ffffff00
inet on backplane (b)  :
host inet (h)          : 192.168.101.30
gateway inet (g)       :
user (u)               : chwe
ftp password (pw) (blank = use rsh):
flags (f)              : 0x0
target name (tn)       : ios2
startup script (s)     :
other (o)              :

[vxWorks boot]: @

boot device            : scsi=3,0
processor number       : 0
host name              : ios
```

56 CHAPTER 4. BOOTING THE TARGET

```
file name              : scsi3://vxWorks/vxWorks
inet on ethernet (e)   : 192.168.101.32:ffffff00
host inet (h)          : 192.168.101.30
user (u)               : chwe
flags (f)              : 0x0
target name (tn)       : ios2
startup script (s)     : /home/chwe/work/book/startup.script

Attaching to scsi device... done.
Loading scsi3://vxWorks/vxWorks...734004
Starting at 0x100000...

Attaching network interface lo0... done.
NFS client support not included.
Loading symbol table from scsi3://vxWorks/vxWorks.sym ...done

]]]]]]]]]]]]]]]]]]]]]]]]]]]]]]]]]]]]]]]
]]]]]]]]]]]]]]]]]]]]]]]]]]]]]]]]]]]]]]]
]]]]]]]]]]]]]]]]]]]]]]]]]]]]]]]]]]]]]
       ]]]]]]]]]] ]]]]    ]]]]]]]]]]      ]]           ]]]]         (R)
]     ]]]]]]]]] ]]]]]]   ]]]]]]]]      ]]           ]]]]
]]     ]]]]]]] ]]]]]]]]  ]]]]]] ]      ]]           ]]]]
]]]     ]]]]] ]   ]]] ]   ]]]] ]]]   ]]]]]]]]]  ]]]] ]] ]]]] ]]  ]]]]]
]]]]    ]]] ]]   ]  ]]]   ]] ]]]]] ]]]]]]    ]] ]]]]]]] ]]]] ]]   ]]]]
]]]]]    ] ]]]]   ]]]]]   ]]]]]]]] ]]]]    ]] ]]]]  ]]]]]]]    ]]]]
]]]]]]    ]]]]]  ]]]]]]   ]  ]]]]] ]]]]   ]] ]]]]   ]]]]]]]]   ]]]]
]]]]]]]    ]]]]] ]   ]]]]]]] ]    ]]]  ]]]]  ]] ]]]]    ]]]] ]]]]   ]]]]
]]]]]]]]  ]]]]]  ]]]  ]]]]]]]     ]    ]]]]]]] ]]]]   ]]]] ]]]] ]]]]]
]]]]]]]]]]]]]]]]]]]]]]]]]]]]]]]
]]]]]]]]]]]]]]]]]]]]]]]]]]]]]]       Development System
]]]]]]]]]]]]]]]]]]]]]]]]]]]]]
]]]]]]]]]]]]]]]]]]]]]]]]]]]]          VxWorks version 5.4
]]]]]]]]]]]]]]]]]]]]]]]]]]              KERNEL: WIND version 2.5
]]]]]]]]]]]]]]]]]]]]]]]]]        Copyright Wind River Systems, Inc., 1984-1998

                    CPU: FORCE COMPUTERS PPC/PowerCore-6604e.  Processor #0.
                    Memory Size: 0x1000000.  BSP version 1.2/1.

->
```

Looks OK! Even though we couldn't find out yet why the double '/' was absolutely necessary. I would suggest making your own test to verify that it also applies to your configuration — or not!

Now, check that we can really access the hard disk:

```
-> cd "scsi3:/"
value = 0 = 0x0
-> mkdir "demo"
value = 0 = 0x0
-> ll
  size        date       time     name
--------    --------   --------  --------
    512    JAN-01-1980 00:00:00  VXWORKS    <DIR>
    512    JAN-01-1980 00:00:00  DEMO       <DIR>
value = 0 = 0x0
->
```

4.1. THE BOOTROM

So, everything looks fine. That is all!

4.1.5 Shared Memory Network

Another, very useful way is to boot using an existing bus system (normally, VME or PCI). In general, any address mapped bus system will do. Why should you not use this existing means for communication if it is there anyway?

The Shared Memory Network is a protocol implementation which allows a network whenever there is at least some shared memory available in the system. How does it work?

Principle of Operation

The Shared Memory Network implements this network, as the name says, via shared memory which is required to be visible to all participating hosts. Normally, the processor board with the processor number 0 makes its memory available. Here, a so-called *anchor* is established. This anchor is a structure that is used as the basis for all the data structures to be used in this network.

Every participating processor is distinguished by its processor number[7]. This number also may determine whether and where the local memory is made available on the bus system. This can be checked in *.../target/config/<BSP>/sysVme.c*: check for calls to **sysProcNumGet()** or in **sysProcNumSet()** in *sysLib.c*. For every participating processor, a data structure is created which describes the access modes, data storage areas and all other necessary information for this specific processor.

Normally, data packets get stored in the master's memory, and the participating processor then takes its data from there or stores its data there.

There is also a definition which allows the use of external memory (e.g. a VMEbus memory card), set up by #define SM_OFF_BOARD. This is also the only instance when you need to set this definition. Normally, as explained before, sm=0xNNNNNNNNN is completely sufficient. If you need to compile in the address, there is a set of definitions in *configAll.h* that is dependent on the CPU family. Also keep in mind you may need to add in the offset for the Bus window mapping (see chapter 5.6.1, page 73 for more!) and review *config.h* for additional information!

For those interested, VxMP also uses this mechanism for communication and to transfer information across the bus system.

For the software running on top of VxWorks, this network looks like another network driver. The Shared Memory Network is used as base for IP; it comes in two different flavors, with or without using a PROXY network.

PROXY network   The PROXY network is enabled if you either choose to #define INCLUDE_PROXY_SERVER in *config.h*, see page 148, or if you choose to elect it in

---
[7] see Chapter 4.1.1 on page 42

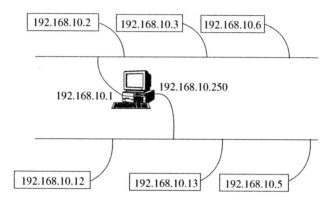

Figure 4.6: Principle of PROXY Network Routing

the project tool. The client functionality is included in the bootrom by default but needs to be enabled by setting a boot flag (see figure 4.1 on page 43). So, if you want to use the PROXY network as a client, you do not need to add anything. You only need to add the definition for the *server*.

PROXY networks allow you to save space in terms of IP addresses: the proxy client requests a packet to be sent from a server, which in turn then requests this packet. By defining this type of networks, transparent network accesses remain necessary. An example configuration is shown in figure 4.6, page 58.

Normal IP network   Normal IP networks use routing to determine how to reach a specific host. To do so, the IP addresses are used, from right to left: a.b.c.d, each number signifying a byte value. a.b.c create a so-called *network*, while d means the node or machine identification. As long as two nodes are on the same network, they can talk to each other directly. If these numbers are different, it needs a router to reach the other machine. This router is also called a *gateway*, as can be set up in the boot parameters. If you need additional routes, you can set them using the command **routeAdd** from the shell prompt or a program.

The same is true for the host; here you need to set up the routes as well, in UNIX and MS Windows using the command *route add* <target IP>[8], <gateway IP> <Max.

---

[8]If the final number of the target IP is a 0, this is assumed to be a whole network

4.2. KERNEL BOOT

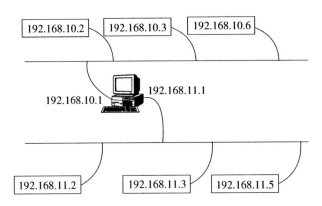

Figure 4.7: Principle of IP Network Routing

Number of Hops>[9].

4.2 Kernel Boot

The next step, after setting up the boot parameters, is the actual boot, i.e. downloading the kernel and then starting it. The kernels have been discussed before, but let us have another look with more internals below.

4.2.1 Standard Kernel — *VxWorks*

This is the actual default kernel of VxWorks. If you use the system as configured by default, you are going to find a kernel prepared for usage with the target server, auto-memory configuration and a basic set of features. If you want to have more included, there are two ways – use the project tool in Tornado II, the configuration tool in Tornado 1.x or edit *config.h*. Never both![10]

To have the older, VxWorks 5.2 shell included, #define CONFIGURATION_5_2. This removes the capabilities of VxWorks 5.3, i.e. the Tornado features. See appendix A on page 139 for more information.

---
[9]UNIX only!
[10]For a more detailed discussion of this topic, see appendix A, page 139.

4.2.2 Standalone Kernel — vxWorks.st

This kernel simply includes the symbol table and has no networking support in it. The result is that, in order to have networking access, you either need to run **usrNetInit()** manually after setting the boot parameters as needed, or to reuse the method of #defineing STANDALONE_NET as described on page 39. Also, the old, target-based shell is included here - no network, no target server connection, unless defined differently.

This is the kernel for final applications which need the possibilities of having a target resident shell and can afford the kernel download but are independent after starting.

4.2.3 Rommable Kernels

A mix of both standalone kernel and the bootrom startup code is the rommable, standalone kernel, called *vxWorks.st_rom* This kernel can be booted directly out of the ROM, with no need for the bootrom.

There are some things to consider. This is again a standalone kernel, meaning that, by default, there is no networking support. The solution using the definition of -DSTANDALONE_NET shown above on page 39 works here, too.

Additionally, the kernel is subject to the uncompression limits of the bootrom, which do not cause any problems there. The ROM contents are copied to RAM and are then unpacked. So, the kernel is unpacked into the local memory at RAM_LOW_ADRS, and then executed from there. If, while coming up, your target stops, this could be the reason: if the area is chosen too small, the unpacked kernel will overwrite the code currently unpacking the kernel...

This will crash!

For some reasons, unpacking the kernel may not be what is wished, but the makefile does not contain rules for the additional target. Nevertheless, there is a simple extension of the file *.../target/config/h/make/rules.bsp* to allow building the non-compressed version. It is quoted in figure 3.3, page 40.

4.3 Common Problems

This chapter discusses common problems when booting the target. Normally, the only result is that - nothing happens. Why could that be? Here is a list of things to check.

- **FTP boot**: is the user set up correctly?

- **FTP boot**: is the FTP service working correctly?
  Try ftp'ing the exact path as defined for the target. Does that work?

- **FTP boot**: is the timeout short enough?

4.3. COMMON PROBLEMS

This is normally signified by the symbol table download failing, usually with error number 0x1a9. Try *rsh* instead or reset the timeout to a lower value.

- **RSH boot**: Do you get the message 'permission denied'?

    Is *.rhosts* or */etc/hosts.equiv* set up correctly? Are file and directory permissions correct? Try executing the command *cat <filename>* from the host machine. In most cases this will fail, and you can find out why.

- **RSH boot**: Check your login shell.

    Is there any unusual output? Is there an stty command? Remove it, or make sure it is only used in interactive shells.

- **General**: Check that the file named exists in the path given.

    Use snoop or another network trace instrument to detect what happens and what messages are coming back to the board trying to download the boot file. Additionally, try to check the validity of the path by using *ls* and, with Copy-Paste, the path as specified in the bootline.

- **Slave Window is not accessible**: Check the mapping.

    Download a kernel built with the same settings as the bootrom to your target system and then use **sysLocalToBusAdrs()** and **sysBusToLocalAdrs()** to find out whether or not the address is really accessible.

Chapter 5

Programming – Writing and Debugging Software

Real-time operating systems are normally used as a base for controlling applications, machines, robotics etc. In this chapter, we will discuss the basic steps of developing software running on top of VxWorks.

In an additional section, we will walk through the different possibilities of constructing and running your application.

5.1 Basic Concepts

VxWorks offers many ways of running your applications. The nice thing is that you can look at the system as something a long the lines of

```
...
main()
{
```

taking care of all the additional things you may need to do in startups. You normally do not need to link your application modules, just download them.

This is also something important to remember with C++ code. Constructors that would be called on program startup need to be called explicitly or code needs to be created using the *ctdt.c* constructor/destructor extraction program *munch*.

5.1.1 Compatibility, Porting

VxWorks supports standard ANSI and K&R C code plus C++. For a more detailed discussion on the compiler see [FSF99b].

Support for other languages like ADA comes either with other companies' add-on tools like Grennhills or can be achieved by building your own version of *gcc*. For more information on this topic, see appendix C.

64   CHAPTER 5. PROGRAMMING

But now, let us start with looking at what comes out of the box with VxWorks.

All necessary include files are delivered. In addition, VxWorks originates from BSD 4.3 UNIX (originally running on SUN 3/60ies and using its includes...), so programs written to run under this operating system and the like are also fairly easy. But there is more to come.

VxWorks offers many additional possibilities like semaphores etc., which were non-standard in those days. Because of this, the include files for these have their own naming convention. It is fairly simple:

- Are we using ANSI C code? – use the 'normal' include file name.

- Are we using UNIX or POSIX code? – try using the 'normal' include file. If that fails, see below.

- Are we using VxWorks specific functions? – try using a fitting name – for instance, **tickGet()** comes from *tickLib.h*, **semGive()** from *semLib.h*, and so on! Looking at the online docs helps...!

As stated before – it is straightforward in *most* cases.

5.2 Programming to Debug

This session is intended to give a comprehensive, general overview on how development using VxWorks works. Important additional considerations are discussed throughout the example.

5.2.1 Example Code

For the following examples, we will use a small piece of sample code as shown below.

```
#include <vxWorks.h>
#include <stdio.h>
#include "tickLib.h"

int mysample(int variable)
{
  int i;

  sysClkRateSet(variable);     /* set system clock rate */
  tickSet(0);                  /* reset system clock */

  printf("running...");        /* show that our program really runs... */

  for (i=0;i<200;i++)
    {
      printf(" %d %d\n", i, tickGet());
```

5.2. PROGRAMMING TO DEBUG

```
        taskDelay(sysClkRateGet()); /* wait a second */
    }
  return i;
}
```

What does this simple code do? It prints the current tick value in 200 lines. That's very simple.

5.2.2 Compiling The Code

Now, after writing it, compile your code. If you #include <vxWorks.h>, you will need to add a -DCPU=PPC604 or something similar to the command line, depending on your target system's CPU type. A reference on the different possible CPU types is found in appendix A.2 on page 157.

Is there anything else?

Yes, you only compile, you do not need to link your code!

So, the very simplest command is as follows:

```
ios $ ccppc -DCPU=PPC604 -g -I$(WIND_BASE)/target/h -c myfirst.c
```

This command will produce a file called *myfirst.o*, an object module. The option '-g' means that debug information is added to the object module. You will need it later. Now, you can download it!

But first a discussion on the mechanism of downloading...

5.2.3 What happens when Downloading Code?

First of all, some points are determined by the way VxWorks treats object modules. When downloading a module, the **ld()** function downloads the module into the target's memory, then checks the module's symbol table for any unresolved functions and compares this against the target's symbol table. Where this symbol table is kept, whether in the target server or on the target, does not make a difference.

Then, if not all missing functions are found, an error message will issued, and the module will be rejected.

Otherwise, the module's symbols will be added to the system's symbol table. The module information can be found using the function **moduleShow()**.

5.2.4 When to link code

The usual question is 'If I don't need to link my code, is there any time when I may need to link it anyway, and how do I do that?'

There are some more general answers to this question.

The paragraph before tells you when you will need to link your modules together - whenever there are interdependencies.

So, let us set up some rules for when linking is really necessary.

- As long as only one module depends on some other module's functions (i.e. a one-way-dependency), that module only needs to be downloaded first.

- When there is a two-or-more-way dependency between modules, they need to be linked together before downloading; otherwise, **ld()** will reject them.

In our case, obviously, you do not need to link your code.

To make life easier, there is a tool called *make* which allows to automate the process of building objects and executables from source code. You can find a short, basic reference in appendix B, page 159.

5.3 Debugging

Now startup your target to be able to test it. To do so, first boot your target. Then, start a target server for your target and, using *launch* or the *IDE* start a *windsh* for it. Then, additionally start *crosswind*.

5.3.1 The *Crosswind* Debugger

Crosswind allows to connect to your target system through the WDB agent and then, remotely, run programs and debug them on a source code level. At the bottom of *Crosswind*, you find GDB, the GNU DebuGger. There is a full manual for it in the GNU Manual, [FSF99a]. It is far more detailed than I could be here. So, look at that reference for all possibilities.

5.3.2 Choosing Your Debug Environment

Before discussing the different environments, let us have a look at how people normally tend to debug their source code, and what that means for the environment afterwards.

Debugging Techniques

The debugging environment is one of the many aspects that have to be chosen. Quite a bunch of experienced programmers still hold on to a technique called "**printf()**-debugging", meaning that you spread **printf()** statements throughout your code and start to look at the statements after the last **printf()** output appearing.

This is certainly a viable way but it does have some shortcomings.

First, and most importantly, you do not know whether the system reached the next **printf()** statement. Why is that? You are working in a multitasking environment. If

5.3. DEBUGGING

your task does something wrong which affects another task which then crashes the system, your task may continue to run longer than it "deserved" to. Or, your output gets queued but not printed on the screen while the system crashes. So, you cannot be sure the problem is really in the area you believe it to be.

Second, littering your code with **printf()**s means that, after debugging, you need to remove them. That is not really easy to do, and – it changes your system's behavior! So, better be careful if you have implicit timing-dependencies (well, you will find out this way...).

A way around removing the **printf()** statements is to create your own pseudo-function which, depending on DEBUG being set is either empty or contains a **printf()** or – even better – **logMsg()** statement.

Why use **logMsg()** instead of **printf()**?

logMsg() is a version of **printf()**, constrained only in the number of arguments taken but being more versatile in the areas where it may be used. This is due to the way **logMsg()** is constructed. The actual command writes its arguments to a message queue that is read from by a low priority task, *tLogTask*. The advantage here is that output can be generated from virtually any place in the program, on interrupt level, in a driver, anywhere. The disadvantage is that, if you crash your program, you will not exactly know where that happened. But that can be achieved using LEDs or low level debuggers once you know the approximate area where things happened. In any case, this guarantees a high level of certainty you can send of the output without disturbing your software.

A Code example outlining the **DEBUGMSG()** practice is shown in figure 5.1.

```
#ifdef DEBUG
#define DEBUGMSG(a,b,c,d,e,f) logMsg(''%s%d%s%s%s%s\n'',__FILE__,\
        __LINE__,a,b,c,d,e,f);
#else
#define DEBUGMSG(a,b,c,d,e,f)
#endif
```

Figure 5.1: Example of Debug Output Code

Another way to debug code is to use a debugger like *Crosswind* as was shown above. This offers the advantage that you can do source-level debugging, running the debugger in your development environment. Additionally, you get many more possibilities to cross-check information like variable-values etc.

Everything usually has a downside to it. What is it here?

First, code size. If you compile using -g, the size of your object code will typically triple. So, it may not fit into memory any more.

Second, system behavior. The system will behave differently with the additional network load or serial interrupts due to the debugger being connected. This may or may not have an impact on your application (we saw applications fail because a faster hard disk was used in the second generation of the system... this is just so you know that there may be a source of future problems here!).

The final way to have a look at this is, when running from the shell, to insert hardware break points. This the purist's style, with nothing between you and your Microprocessor.

Upside: total control, of course.

Downside: today's processors have really awkward assembly languages... there is no such thing as source level debugging available. If you like it, fine, but it is very probable you will not. Additionally, there are some processors which do not fully support hardware breakpoints.

Host-Based vs. Target-Based Tools

As stated before, there are two different toolsets in VxWorks. First, the ones which comprise Tornado, *windsh* etc., running on the host. Additionally, "for the fans of old-school", there are the originally delivered, pre-Tornado tools. Why? After all, this was stone age!

There is a very simple answer to this question — both have their merits. The host-based tools are easy-to-use tools with many advantages discussed before, but they have some prerequisites which need to be fulfilled. The target-based tools can always be made available. First a discussion of what is necessary to run the host-based toolset, second, in what cases it is more sensible to use the target-based tools. In short - a summary.

When the Host-based tools can run This is fairly simple. The host-based toolset requires a connection between the target server and the target system. That can be achieved via netrom, a serial line, or, more commonly, via the network. If this connection is available, the host-based toolset will work.

If, due to whatever reason, the target system can not be connected to the host, using the target based tools has to be considered. One possible reason is system load. I have seen a system where a connection using the target server communication ended in a system hang-up because the system load exceeded 100 %.

Target-based Tools They are always available whenever a standalone kernel is created. So, better have a look at what they can do and what they cannot! The shell offers *vi*-like command line editing[1], a C-interpreter and more — but no TCL interpreter. Also keep in mind that the C interpreter is set up pretty simple - it will treat all non-floating point numbers as `integer`, floating point as `double`. That may create havoc in some comparisons, so be sure to cast correctly!

---

[1] *vi* is really simple - there are two modes, *insert* and *command* mode. Command mode is entered using the `ESC` key, insert mode using the `i` (insert here) or `a` (append after character) key. A means *append at the end of the line*, `x` deletes the character below the cursor, h takes you left, l right, j up, k down (look at these characters as a cross on the keyboard!).

5.4 C++ AND VXWORKS

Also keep in mind that you may create a memory leak when playing around on the shell: `printf(``test'')` will finish properly but leave the space for ``test'' allocated behind!

Additionally, even in a networked environment – if, due to not really bug-free circumstances, the network becomes unavailable, a target based shell still remains available, the host-based version however disappears or needs to be replaced by a serial connection.

> Something to consider is that someone else could also make use of this connection. I remember someone on a mailing list who found a serial interface with an open shell on it and was asking how to use it...!
> So, keep in mind if you are not the only one with access to the machine – password protection might be a good idea, too.
> And you should know there is a default password set in *configAll.h*!

Wrap-Up To summarize: there are cases where the host-based tools are not available. Then, the most essential functions are available via the target based tools. It is your decision what to go for, target based tools, a serial or a network connection.

5.4 C++ and VxWorks

As of Tornado, VxWorks includes the abilities you need to start development using C++[2]. The system delivers the C++ Standard Library; Template support has been enhanced compared to the standard *gcc 2* compiler family. If you need a very up-to-date snapshot, contact your WRS FAE.

How does VxWorks handle C++ constructors[3] and destructors[4]?

The handling of global constructors and destructors is handled using the program *munch* which is executed when building the kernel. This program searches the object modules for constructors and destructors which need to be executed on startup/shutdown. They are then placed in the file *ctdt.c*. This file is compiled into the kernel and executed on system startup/shutdown. Shutdown methods are usually there – but a real time system should never shut down!

5.4.1 Wind Foundation Classes

The add-on Wind Foundation Classes offer example wrapper classes for the VxWorks kernel. They are neither complete nor do they claim to be. They are simply a few examples of how you might want to encapsulate the O/S facilities.

---

[2] In the early days, additional Centerline tools allowed for C++ development, which created some overhead – this was all based on the old AT&T cfront preprocessor solution!

[3] method (function) which is executed when an object is created e.g. using **new()**

[4] method executed upon destruction of an object e.g. using **delete()**

5.4.2 tools.h++ and Booch Classes

These additional – now obsolete – add-on packages allow for the usage of the additional OO methods. If you want to make use of them for better portability and encapsulation, this is certainly something to have a closer look at.

Finally, there are several good starting points for C++ based development. Something to keep in mind, though: in most cases, you need to develop your own class schema and your own setup. So, in most cases it is better to simply start from scratch than using additional tools. But, if you want to make use of them, they are there!

5.5 Starting and Running your Application

The big issue today is - "OK, I've got a kernel and I've got an application. But how do I bind them together and start them, especially if I need to be situation-dependent?" This is what this chapter is about. It cannot give you all answers, but it can give some hints where to look for solutions to this problem.

5.5.1 Big Block - ONE package doing it All...

This is the easy way. Simply add your application to LIB_EXTRA in the *Makefile*, and it will automatically be added to the kernel. You need to start it though.

Starting your application is achieved setting the corresponding #defines in *usrApplInit.c*. The example code gets called in *usrConfig.c* at the end of the **usrRoot()** function as shown in figure 5.2.

```
#ifdef INCLUDE_USER_APPL
    /* Startup the user's application */

    USER_APPL_INIT;    /* must be a valid C statement or block */
#endif
```

Figure 5.2: Excerpt from *usrConfig.c*, User Application start code

The code in *usrApplInit.c*, usually found in your project directory is listed in figure 5.3, page 71.

The advantage of this approach is that there will be no time-consuming additional downloads, no undefined externals, no additional problems due to missing network connections etc.

The shortcoming of it is however that the initial download of the kernel may be fairly time consuming. Also, if using a compressed kernel, decompression space and time need to be considered. Sometimes, there is no time for such luxury. But uncompressed kernels tend to be huge!

5.5. STARTING AND RUNNING YOUR APPLICATION

```
/*****************************************************************
*
* usrAppInit - initialize the users application
*/
void usrAppInit (void)
    {
#ifdef  USER_APPL_INIT
        USER_APPL_INIT;            /* for backwards compatibility */
#endif

    /* add application specific code here */
    }
```

Figure 5.3: Code excerpt from *usrApplInit.c* – where application startup code should be inserted

In addition, there is no such thing as runtime configuration. Or, you are always downloading a huge overhead application which you do not need. Also, ROM space may become an issue due to the overall size.

This may be a viable solution, but not for every problem.

5.5.2 Startup Scripts

Special startups, dynamic setups and automatic execution of a lot of commands without having to compile are the domain of startup scripts. These also allow for very fast changes in the setup procedure of the system.

To use startup scripts, you need the target resident shell and you need to include the option #define INCLUDE_STARTUP_SCRIPT. Then you need to use the bootrom parameter *startup script* to make use of the feature. Remember, though, that you may not be able to set the parameters in the NVRAM if you are using a rommable kernel and will need to set them either by compiling them in as needed or by changing the **sysNvRamGet()** function which is definitely not recommended.

5.5.3 Dynamically Loading Applications and Starting Them

The startup script as discussed above may also be used to download and run user applications. This is the way if you have only limited space and need to run applications depending on external events.

Another way would be to download applications from a program, find the entry symbol (that is the name of the function you will call first in the downloaded code module) in the symbol table and call the startup function using the pointer obtained using **symFindByName()**. To be able to do this, you will need the target resident symbol table.

5.5.4 Usual Problems

Missing Functions

A usual issue when porting software is that, when downloading on a PowerPC (and sometimes other architectures, too), you may see messages about missing functions that...

- are not available on your target system
- you did not create in your code
- have very unusual names and start with _underlines!

What happened?

Very simple! probably you compiled a program that still has the function **main()** in it. *Gcc* is a nice compiler that will immediately create all the surrounding code around this function in order to be able to start the program after it is completely linked to *crt0.o* and *crti.o*, the files that contain the startup and clean up code for "normal" operating systems.

In VxWorks, you do not need (and have) this! And that is your problem. If you rename **main()** to **mymain()**, everything will be alright.

Downloaded, Unreachable Functions

This may be an issue in older or speed-optimized PowerPC systems. The result is that you get strange error messages downloading code or that successfully download code cannot be started.

How can that happen?

The reason behind this is the PowerPC architecture. It is built for virtual-memory based systems and does not take into account large-memory systems with a VxWorks-style uniform, linear memory model. Due to this design decision, PowerPC can do relative jumps only with 24 bit addresses, resulting in a memory border at 32 MB. If you have to jump further, this may fail. Today's *gcc* has a flag called *-flong-call* that takes care of this by loading the target address into a register and then jumping indirectly. However, there may be older libraries out there that cannot do this, and, as this mechanism takes time, you might not want to waste so much time.

Usually, though, with processor speed growing every day, this should not be an issue any more. Anyway, it is important to know!

5.6 Programming VME and PCI devices

An important topic of programming target systems is programming of specific devices. In today's modern applications, many systems contain sub-bus systems to allow for easy extension and expansion of the system's abilities.

5.6. PROGRAMMING VME AND PCI DEVICES

That is the reason why bus systems are used and how to program them will be discussed here. Additionally, the question whether or not to add a driver to access devices needs a closer look.

5.6.1 Bus Devices

Buses are usually memory-mapped, determining through the address which device is addressed. In addition, buses have the characteristics of having a defined endian-ness. For example, the VMEbus is big-endian, while PCI is little endian. Depending on the endian-ness of the processor used in the specific application, byte-swapping is absolutely necessary.

Normally, if this is necessary, the BSPs provide functions for this. Hardware also has some features to help here.

BSP Mappings

Depending on your BSP type, there are several ways to determine the actual mapping.

Generally spoken, VxWorks is based on a "physical = virtual" addressing scheme. That means, if your manual says that device A is at physical address 0x10101010, chances are high you will actually find it there, even using virtual addressing, as is usual in today's workstation processors.

To verify this, you should look out for one of two files, both located in the actual BSP directory. The file to look for is called *memDesc.c*. If this file is not available, have a look at *sysLib.c*. This file contains a two-dimensional array called **sysPhys-MemDesc**, which contains the information to be stored in the actual MMU[5] tables. This way, here you can look up what is mapped, and where.

```
{
(void *) LOCAL_MEM_LOCAL_ADRS,
(void *) LOCAL_MEM_LOCAL_ADRS,
RAM_LOW_ADRS,
VM_STATE_MASK_VALID | VM_STATE_MASK_WRITABLE |
VM_STATE_MASK_CACHEABLE | VM_STATE_MASK_MEM_COHERENCY,
VM_STATE_VALID        | VM_STATE_WRITABLE       |
VM_STATE_CACHEABLE_NOT | VM_STATE_MEM_COHERENCY
},
```

The different fields – we will show the entry quoted above line-by-line – have the following meanings:

The first line gives the address as seen from the local CPU.

```
{
(void *) LOCAL_MEM_LOCAL_ADRS,
```

---

[5]Memory Management Unit - Hardware "processor" that manages memory accesses from the CPU, memory mappings – i.e. what is found where – and may translate accesses from the CPU to the actual DRAM location

Then, the MMU mapping entry is set up. VxWorks loves the "physical=virtual" address setup, so this will normally be identical. Additionally, this is set up in a format fit for the MMU. For PowerPC, this is identical to the address as seen from the CPU.

```
(void *) LOCAL_MEM_LOCAL_ADRS,
```

Now, the size for this mapping has to be set up.

```
RAM_LOW_ADRS,
```

What else is left? Simple: options for the respective page. As VxWorks mappings are static, here you determine the MMU mask of what actually can be set up.

```
VM_STATE_MASK_VALID | VM_STATE_MASK_WRITABLE |
VM_STATE_MASK_CACHEABLE | VM_STATE_MASK_MEM_COHERENCY,
```

Here, the real definition takes place - what is enabled (that was allowed earlier). If you miss allowing a setup in the line before and then try to select it here, it will not be set!

```
VM_STATE_VALID         | VM_STATE_WRITABLE       |
VM_STATE_CACHEABLE_NOT | VM_STATE_MEM_COHERENCY
},
```

Other Mapping Possibilities

Today, besides the MMU setup, there are additional registers included in the chips to allow a quicker access to some necessary resources. This, for instance, in PowerPCs is done using the so-called BAT[6] registers.

The reason for this is that normally there is only space for the most recently used memory page entries in the MMU. If this memory is used up, or a requested address is not available in these pages, the MMU will set up a table in local memory. If an address is requested from a location which is currently not remapped in the MMU, the MMU needs to go out to memory and start a 'table walk' to search for the correct address area. As this, basically, means the MMU has to execute memory reads, and several of them, this means quite some loss of time.

Additionally, MMUs are normally organized in pages of a fixed size. This may mean quite a few entries in case of today's usual 4GB address space, cut into 4kB sized pages...

And that is the reason these registers exist!

They will be set up separately from the **sysPhysMemDesc()** setup, usually either in a special file (e.g. *sysBat.c*), or in an additional structure in *sysLib.c*.

---

[6]Block Address Translation

5.6. PROGRAMMING VME AND PCI DEVICES

Bridges

Bridges translate between two buses; these buses can be different or not. Examples for bridges are Tundra Universe, FORCE FGA-5x00 or SUN S4, translating between VME and PCI, or chips like DEC (now Intel) 21554 or FORCE's Sentinel^{TM}, a PCI-to-PCI bridge.

Mapping mechanism via bridges

The example shown here is the mapping of VMEbus devices. We will neglect in-between bridges as you would experience in a PowerPC based system, because they virtually disappear from the programmer's view.

Address Range	VME Address Space	Local Start Address	VME Start Address	Window Size
1	A32	0x80000000	MASTER_BASE_ADRS	768 MB
2	A24	0xfd000000	0x000000	16 MB
3	A16	0xfe000000	0x0000	64 kB

Table 5.1: Example for a VME mapping – Default Setup for PowerCore

As of Tornado 1.01, MASTER_BASE_ADRS has been replaced by the definition of VME_A32_MSTR_LOCAL in *config.h*.

The idea behind the setup is that, as shown in figure 5.4 on page 76, a given area of the VMEbus[7] is mapped into the space visible to the local CPU. The area of VME space visible locally depends on both system architecture and time requirements by the user's application — bigger mappings take longer! To overcome this, use BAT registers where available as described before.

So how do I find out which address I need to access a given VMEbus address?

Fairly simple. For the standard setup, or for a setup based on changes to the #defines in *config.h*, simply use the function **sysBusToLocalAdrs()** to determine where the address is mapped:

```
-> foo=0
new symbol "foo" added to symbol table
foo = <address>: value= 0 = 0x0
-> sysBusToLocalAdrs(0x0d, 0x10000,&foo)
value = 0 = 0x0
-> foo
value = <where the address is mapped>
```

---

[7] You cannot map the whole of VME in a 32bit based system, as the overall addressable space is limited to 4 GB, whereas VMEbus A32 alone already comprises of 4GB. So, there is a certain windowing-approach which hides areas from the programmer's view. This may create a problem, though!

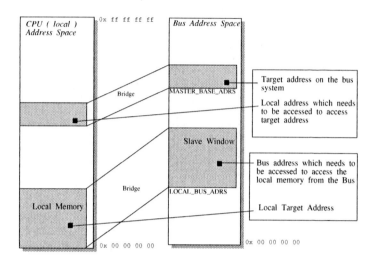

Figure 5.4: Accessing Addresses on Bus Systems - Principle

Now, try the same for an address which is *not* accessible:

```
-> foo=0
foo = <address>: value= 0 = 0x0
-> sysBusToLocalAdrs(0x0d, 0x1000000,&foo)
value = -1 = 0xffffffff
```

As you can see, the function returns either OK (i.e. 0x0) if the address is accessible or ERROR (i.e. -1) if it is not.

Also, the so-called *slave window* allows accesses from VME into the local memory. The accesses into local memory depend on the address the local memory is mapped to[8]. And, to allow the user to find out where an address is mapped to, you have the counter-function to the one named above, called **sysLocalToBusAdrs()**.

Again, an example which is accessible – assuming we had a reboot before so foo is unknown again:

```
-> foo=0
new symbol "foo" added to symbol table
foo = <address>: value= 0 = 0x0
```

---

[8]Be warned! For some BSPs, this mapping not only depends on the Processor Number – even the enabling of the slave window is Processor Number dependent. Check the **sysProcNumSet()** source code in *sysLib.c* for its according setup!

5.6. PROGRAMMING VME AND PCI DEVICES

```
-> sysLocalToBusAdrs(0x0d, 0x10000,&foo)
value = 0 = 0x0
-> foo
foo = <address>: value= <wherever the address is visible on the bus>
```

As you can see, this is nearly identical to the previous access. But do not confuse the different directions! Now, try the same for an address which is *not* accessible:

```
-> foo=0
value = 0 = 0x0
-> sysLocalToBusAdrs(0x0d, 0x1000000,&foo)
value = -1 = 0xffffffff
```

The return value tells us what is OK and what is not. Again, do not confuse the direction. This may have unexpected results...

5.6.2 Programming Devices

So, here we are. You have set up the mapping. You have enabled the ranges on all bridges you need to be able to access your device. Maybe you have also executed the configuration cycles to enable the mapping. Fine! What is next??

First, some thought!

To cleanly map a device, the best way is to create a structure or object which maps the device's registers into the application. This way, the code becomes a lot more readable. You sould know about one possible caveat: Compilers tend to 'optimize' the alignment of structures to allow for better access. If you really need a specific setup, check the compiler manual to see what you can do about this.

Also, look at the way the compiler handles **packed** structures.

Something else to look at is what the processor needs. Due to today's caching structures, some processors need accesses or reads only on 64 bit borders or some other constraints. That may mean you may need some padding before or after the structure.

After setting up the structure, point it to the location of the chip and execute your code.

Additionally there should also be some function to read the device's register set and display it — you will love that for debugging your code! Anyway, let us start with a checklist of what is necessary to properly program a device.

Preparations

First of all, you need to get all the setup information on the device you require to program it. What is that?

When crossing buses, find out the correct addresses. Additionally, you should know the endian-ness of the device compared to the endian-ness of your host processor. It may be different, with the difference handled by a bridge, or it may not be handled at all. Additionally, it might be a good idea (if you want to stay portable) to have a function set included which will or will not do byte swapping, depending on the endian-ness via functions declared **inline**. That will make sure they are placed in your final code, not addressed via jumps if they are needed, and will simply be eliminated if they are not needed.

You also need all information to have access to the device, mappings and probing information so you can not only access the device but also make sure you are really talking to the device you believe you are talking to.

Then, you also need the register setup information and create a structure for it. Additionally, `#defines` should be set up for all important bits. This will not only make your code a lot more readable, it also reduces the issue of errors being coded due to incorrect register settings.

Startup

So finally we now know...

- where the device is located

- how to find out it actually is the device we want to program

- the register setup and all important bit settings

And now?

If you want to keep the routines really portable, you should now start with an initialization function which sets up a structure that describes the device, and maybe also initializes the device.

The static description structure should consist of a pointer to the actual device, an initialization status and an additional **void** pointer for extension purposes. This is the point at which you should consider whether or not there may be several identical devices in the system. If the answer is "yes", this structure should either be part of a linked list, or it should have some other way of keeping track of the devices it talks about. It also should ensure you have certain access to exactly the device you are talking about. Using the declaration **static** under these circumstances may create some issues because then all tasks will have access to exactly the same global information. This may or may not be desired, depending on your design.

Your initialization function should take the actual device address as parameters (here you need the address; everything else should only use indirect addressing!), and possibly general information, depending on the device.

Once this is achieved, you should create the register dump function to check what you did to the device, and what the effect is. This is really device dependent now.

5.6. PROGRAMMING VME AND PCI DEVICES

The Real Work

What is called the real work, now entirely depends on you. What you need to do with the device, should be done. If the preparations were made in a clean manner, this means that the code created now is very readable and very close to self-explaining (which does not mean it does not need documentation, though!). It just means that debugging the code should really be a lot easier to do.

And then, once the raw format is reached, of course, there is the most interesting task of all – debugging. And that is what the next step is all about.

Trouble Shooting Device Programming

This section discusses what may go wrong and what to do to troubleshoot it.

Bus Analyzer If you are working on bus devices frequently, a bus analyzer may be a good idea. That way, you can directly monitor the accesses generated by your program and look at what is really happening. This helps to find a lot problems generated in this environment.

But now, let us have a look at what usually happens.

Compiler The compiler may pack the structure differently than expected. This is a common error. Make sure you *really* got what you believed you got! This can be done by reading the assembly code generated[9]. There may also be compiler error events. Again, check the assembly language as a last resort to find out what really happend. This can also be done from the shell using the *l* command so you get complete resolution of the symbols.

Processor and Out-Of-Order Execution There is another caveat to take care of: Especially with the PowerPC but also with other RISC processors you may see out-of-order execution of commands, resulting in an incorrect order of commands being executed. Here, to ensure proper execution, you need to use the assembly language command `eieio`, enforce instruction execution in order. If your processor can do out-of-order execution, there will be a similar command there. Basically, this enforces the execution of all commands in the processor's pipelines before executing the next command. The pipelines will be re-loaded at this point, so you may need to issue this command frequently. Why not do this at all times? Because it slows down the processor a lot and also changes timing! There are several execution and math units running parallel, executing code. Using this command, you will empty all pipelines before proceeding!

---
[9]Hint: for *gcc*, the command line option to get assembly language is -S!

Bridges Also, you need to make sure that you do not see byte accesses being accumulated into burst accesses or bigger accesses which may be done by a bridge chip. If your target device cannot bear this, it will – even though in principle your program is doing the correct thing – kill your desired goal. Also, there is the possibility that read accesses are bypassing writes – resulting in you reading the register before your write command that you want to check is executed...! This is not just theory, it really happens!

The next chapter will look at drivers in general. It extends the general device programming part found here into portability issues and design decision issues.

5.7 VxWorks Additional Devices – Drivers

For VxWorks two different concepts may be used to access additional devices. This is covered in [WRS97], a class certainly to be considered for driver and BSP developers. This subsection is intended to give a short overview over the respective aspects.

5.7.1 The Driver Concept of VxWorks

A short description of this is found in [WRS99i]. There are two basically different ways of accessing external or internal devices in VxWorks.

First, there is an application-specific way, using a library for access through device specific functions. This enables the programmer to totally tailor the code to the application. If you want to use standard software or port the code to a different platform, you will face the following problems:

- Non-portable device access due to alignment, addresses etc. being hard coded
- Platform-dependent code
- Additional efforts if a driver for the specific device actually exists on the new platform

On the other hand, the library-code way ensures many benefits, while most of the problems stated above can be worked around with a little thought. To stay portable, you should have a look at chapter 5.9, page 90. The advantages are task-tailored code with little overhead and no additional, unnecessary functionality.

Second, there is the UNIX-like standard driver concept. This allows creating drivers which offer standard interfaces like **open()**, **close()**, **read()**, **write()** and **ioctl()**. Some even may offer facilities like **select()**. These drivers may create some additional overhead on creation at first, but once they exist, they offer a more portable access mode if written in a clean way.

5.7. VXWORKS ADDITIONAL DEVICES – DRIVERS 81

Especially, from a software point of view, this means that standard mechanisms like STREAMS and normal device I/O can be used. If necessary, for first testing runs, you may even substitute a different, known to work, device instead. This enables additional advantages for fast lane starts in development.

Disadvantages? Sure. Everything making life easier is bought with one or more downsides. In this case, it is time in terms of the VxWorks I/O system overhead. You will certainly need some time to get through the I/O system to your driver. If you can spare this time, fine. If not, you had better resort to your driver library.

Additionally, if your device is not really an I/O device (e.g. a digital I/O card), it is probably too much overhead, if you only want to set a bit, to do **open()**, **write()** and **close()**. Here, a library-style driver would certainly be a more reasonable choice.

A simple Example Driver

So, let us look at a simple example driver. This driver is taken from the Wind River's Device drivers Class, so do not worry if you recognize it there.

It has been weeded out to avoid too much confusion while discussing the different parts of the driver. Again, this is an example that is used to outline how the different functions work. For a complete discussion, visit the training! It is worth it.

The DAADIO is an external card that was used in the lab that carries the actual PIO device (Parallel IO). This allows to simply connect an LED or connect one port to another to get results.

The header file, below, contains all information in two blocks. The public part is what is deliberately made visible to the outside. The private part normally should not even be cared about. Personally, I would even move this into a separate file to hide it from curious eyes.

```
#include "pioLib.h"
#include "iosLib.h"
#include "ioLib.h"
/******************************************************
                    PUBLIC
******************************************************/

/* ioctl commands */
#define IS_ON            0
#define IS_OFF           1

[...]

/******************************************************
                    PRIVATE
******************************************************/
typedef struct
        {
```

CHAPTER 5. PROGRAMMING

```
            DEV_HDR       devHdr;
            int           port;
          } PIO_DEV;

typedef struct
          {
            PIO_DEV  *pDev;
            int      channel;
          } PIO_CH;
```

The actual C file contains the functions needed for the driver to work properly plus additional functions that may be needed internally. Some external functions are defined in an external library *pioLib.o*.

The preable of the driver file sets the stage, including importing, i.e. referencing external variables that are needed to run the device.

Note, that pioDrvNum is set to ERROR here. So, if you reload the driver, this may or may not be overwritten!

To allow the links to the respective functions in **pioDrv()**, all external function names need to be declared before the actual initialization function. They will be linked into the driver system as part of this function.

```
#include "pioDrv.h"

IMPORT DAADIO daadio;
IMPORT PIO pio;
LOCAL int pioDrvNum = ERROR;

/* forward declarations */
int pioOpen();
STATUS pioClose();
int pioRead();
int pioWrite();
int pioIoctl();
```

pioDrv() is the initialization function for the device. Its task is to ensure all prerequisites are met, the device is present etc. etc. Then, it will link the functions into the VxWorks driver table.

```
STATUS pioDrv(base, intLevel, intVector)
    char *   base;
    int      intLevel;
    int      intVector;
    {

    if (daadio.initialized == FALSE)
       {
       if (daadioInit(base, intLevel, intVector) == ERROR)
           return (ERROR);
       }
```

5.7. VXWORKS ADDITIONAL DEVICES - DRIVERS 83

```
        if (pio.initialized == FALSE)
            {
            if (pioInit(0) == ERROR)
                return (ERROR);
            }

            if (pioDrvNum==ERROR)
            {
                    if((pioDrvNum=iosDrvInstall(
                                    pioOpen, NULL, pioOpen, pioClose,
                                    pioRead,pioWrite,pioIoctl)
                            )==ERROR)
                            return ERROR;
            }

        return (OK);
        }
```

From now on, things are very device specific. So, only the generic functions are discussed.

pioDevCreate() is the function that creates a "device" that makes the actual device accessible through the driver system. So, after **pioDevCreate()**, you can run a normal fd=open("/pio",0) command to gain access to the device.

Note here, that the function first re-checks that the initialization has been completed and all parameters passed to it are in range. Otherwise, you may get unpredictable results either accessing non-existent ports or using a device name with no driver associated to it.

```
STATUS pioDevCreate(char* name, int port, BOOL mode)
    {
    PIO_DEV *       pPioDev;
    UINT8           portBit;
    UINT8 *         pOutputEnablePort;
    UINT8 *         pPort;

    if (pioDrvNum == ERROR)
        {
        printf ("pioDrv() must be called first\n");
        return (ERROR);
        }
    if (port < PORT_A || port >= PIO_MAX_PORTS)
        {
        printf ("Invalid port number: %d\n", port);
        return (ERROR);
        }

    /* ....... ???     ....... */

    }
```

Now, the functions below implement the real functions of the driver. They do the actual work if you call **open()**, **close()**, **read()**, **write()** and **ioctl()**.

The **open()** function has to check access rights if applicable and ensure you get access to the correct port.

```
int pioOpen(DEV_HDR* pDevHdr, char* name, int mode)
    {
    /* .......  ???       ....... */

    }
```

The **close()** function's task is to clean up after doing I/O, release memory used internally if applicable and do all the other tasks as needed.

```
STATUS pioClose (int devId)
    {
    /* .......  ???       ....... */

    return (OK);
    }
```

read() and **write()** are the functions that really do something. They are generic functions, so they always accept buffers with variable size and also return how many bytes were read or written, even if, as in this case, the device is only a bit device! That is the reason why they return a hard-coded 1 here. Otherwise, make sure they hit the real values.

```
pioRead(int devId, char* buf, int nBytes)
    {
    PIO_CH *  pCh;
    BOOL      value;

    /* .......  ???       ....... */

    return (1);
    }

pioWrite(int devId, char* buf, int nBytes)
    {
    PIO_CH *  pCh;

    /* .......  ???       ....... */

    return (1);
    }
```

5.8. INTERRUPTS IN VXWORKS

The most interesting function is **ioctl()**. As it takes device specific commands, you may do anything you like in it. Someone even used **ioctl()** to transfer data...! This is certainly not the way it is intended to be used.

Normally, this function should only be used to set or get parameters and execute control functions. For I/O, **read()** and **write()** are more suitable.

```
pioIoctl(int devId, int cmd, int arg)
    {
    switch (cmd)
        {
        case IS_ON:
            status = pioGet (port, channel);
            if (arg)
                *(int *)arg = status;
            break;
        case IS_OFF:
            status = !pioGet (port, channel);
            if (arg)
                *(int *)arg = status;
            break;
[...]
        default:
            errnoSet (S_ioLib_UNKNOWN_REQUEST);
            status = ERROR;
            break;
        }
    return (status);
    }
```

This is all there is to be said about simple drivers. Again, for specifics, visit the class.

5.8 Interrupts in VxWorks

Interrupts are a method for asynchronous notification of processes. Additionally, the system-dependency of interrupts and their handling have implications on the real-time behaviour of a real-time system. This fact makes it so important that it needs its own section. This one.

Interrupt requests also carry the short name IRQ, from Interrupt ReQuest.

They are a hardware facility which does exactly what the name says – it interrupts the processor's execution of a specific task to allow for execution of the Interrupt Service Routines (ISR). This makes reaction to sudden events very easy, but also has some drawbacks which need to be mentioned here as well.

The disadvantage of this very handy method is that interrupts stop the system from continuing with its current work. So, the main design goal is to keep ISRs as short as possible. The shortest version (which should not be exceeded too far unless absolutely necessary) looks like figure 5.5, below.

```
void handleIRQ()
{
    int register* = REG_ADRS;      /* This register needs to be written to*/
                                   /* to acknowledge the IRQ and reset it */

    semGive (notificationSem);     /* notify my task an interrupt occurred */

    *register=CLEAR_EVENT;         /* Clear the register to allow new     */
                                   /* interrupts to occur                 */

    return;                        /* Done!                               */
}
```

Figure 5.5: Example for an ideal Interrupt Service Routine, ISR

The reason is that, while the system handles this interrupt, it can do nothing else, even though, maybe another, more important interrupt needs to be serviced. This simply locks up the whole system.

Interrupts may – and that is very system dependent – be interrupted by higher-level interrupts, which may cause additional problems. Something to keep in mind if developing drivers!

Normally, the Interrupt Service Routine should do the same as above and then transfer the control to a task of the appropriate priority level - high if it is very important, low if it is not so – but, anyway, make sure the task actually runs fairly soon!

5.8.1 VMEbus Interrupts

The basic way of handling interrupts in VxWorks stems from the VxWorks history. It was created to work on embedded, industrial systems based on VMEbus and 68000 interrupts. This is the reason why VME interrupts are discussed at large up front. Every interrupt source is assigned its own unique interrupt number, sometimes also called interrupt vector [10]. In this text, as in many other places as well, you will find both interrupt vector and interrupt number used without making a distinction. The background is that, in fact, the interrupt vector is the machine level representation of the interrupt number!

To understand the way things work, let us have a look at VME interrupts.

---

[10] For PCI bus systems, this is not true any more. Here, due to only four interrupt lines available on PCI, there can be multiple ISRs (Interrupt Service Routines) assigned to one vector. Anyway, this will be covered on page 89!

5.8. INTERRUPTS IN VXWORKS

VMEbus Interrupts — Background

VMEbus interrupts work as follows:

Step 1 The interrupter pulls a line to request an interrupt from the interrupt handler on a specific level. This line is chained to slot 1.

Step 2 The board in slot 1 finds that the Interrupt Request Line for the level specified is pulled and then has two options:

- If this board does not handle interrupts at all or is not enabled to handle this interrupt level, it passes the interrupt request to the next board (Interrupt Daisy Chain).
- If this board is enabled to handle interrupts for this level, it will pull the Interrupt Acknowledge Line and ...

Step 3 The board starts the Interrupt Acknowledge Cycle. It reads the interrupt vector from the VMEbus presented by the interrupter, an 8-bit value used to identify which Interrupt Service Routine is to be run.

So, the interrupt vector really serves the main task of connecting an interrupt source to the appropriate handler.

But, there are other types of interrupts as well.

Mailboxes or Location Monitors   Mailboxes[11] are a way of notifying a specific VMEbus board without using VMEbus interrupts but still having the advantage of the asynchronous effect on the target board. So, what happens?

A mailbox works in the following way: when a specific location on VME is accessed from VME, this triggers an interrupt on the board accessed. Where this access needs to take place, and how it has to be executed is documented in the manual of the VMEbus bridge, delivered by the respective manufacturer.

This mechanism allows an asynchronous notification which only appears as one single normal access on the VMEbus, thus leaving bandwidth to other issues.

Watchdogs   A watchdog timer is an interrupt source that needs to be re-triggered regularly. If this does not happen, the watchdog will execute a pre-defined function, e.g. execute an NMI or pull RESET.

What does this mean? Basically, by requiring a retrigger on a regular basis, the watchdog ensures that the system stays at least sane enough to execute the triggering function. If this is not true anymore, the system needs to be sent into a defined state, usually the Power-Up state.

---

[11] This term is used for both Mailboxes and Location Monitors – especially because there is little difference between Mailboxes and Location Monitors – only that Mailboxes (sometimes) allow for storage of a value. See your documentation for specifics.

There are two different types of watchdogs, software and hardware versions. The software version usually offers more functionality but less security (what if your system is corrupted enough for the software watchdog not to work anymore?). The hardware version usually only allows setting very few parameters and then, upon execution will either create an NMI or a RESET.

Now, let us have a closer look at the internals of the system.

5.8.2 Interrupt Internals

This is closer to the hardware – what does an interrupt do in general? [12]

Interrupt Service Functions and How They Get Called

An Interrupt Input Line is a signal line connected to the CPU. If an interrupt occurs, this line is pulled to a different, pre-defined signal level.

There are two different type of interrupts, level- and edge-sensitive interrupts. *Level-sensitive* interrupts mean that, after handling an interrupt, the ISR will be called again as long as the line remains active. An *edge-sensitive* interrupt input will create the interrupt every time the signal line is pulled to the respective edge.

After an interrupt line is pulled, the CPU will start to run the connected Interrupt Service Routine. This normally is a generic function which then will determine the source of the interrupt and execute the specific ISR for the respective source using a so-called Interrupt Vector . This interrupt vector is used as index into the table of available interrupt service routines to start the appropriate function to handle the interrupt. E.g. for VME, the vector is physically transmitted as part of the IACK (Interrupt Acknowledge) Cycle. This part is architecture- and implementation dependent.

An ISR is connected to a specific Interrupt Vector using **intConnect()**, a VxWorks System function.

Now, the ISR has to handle the actual interrupt. To do so, as we know who created the interrupt, we will check for the interrupt source's status, fetch or transmit data and re-enable the interrupt. Then, finish the ISR and return control to the operating system. Everything else should be done on task-, not interrupt level to prevent system locks or race conditions. If something goes wrong while you are at interrupt level, there is no safeguard available! The only safety-belt could be using a hardware watchdog. But that may not be available everywhere! So, ensure the IRQ routine really and only does what is expected. Anything that is not absolutely necessary to be done on IRQ level, should be executed on task level.

Additionally, problems at interrupt level are very difficult to debug as there is no real way to check what is going on. That problem is also cured by running most of what needs to be done after the interrupt at a high task level, with a task waiting for the appropriate signal.

---

[12]Hardware-people forgive me — this is not totally correct but gives some of the background of what happens in a given system!

5.8. INTERRUPTS IN VXWORKS

This is what you *should* do. Now, let's look at the other side...

What You Must Not Do

Interrupt Service Routines may occur any time. That includes moments where the system is busy doing other tasks – after all that is why interrupts were invented. Because interrupt level is a peculiar system state, ISR may do only a few things.

This results in the fact that functions that create interrupts themselves like **printf()** must not be used in this context. A list of allowed libraries and some functions can be found in [WRS99j].

Usage of disallowed functions may have two results.

One is simply instability of the system. This means that the ISR may work a thousand times but will fail eventually. This is very difficult to track but happens very rarely.

The usual response to usage of a disallowed function is a hanging system. Very simple, is it not?

5.8.3 PCIbus Interrupts – What's the Difference?

There are several differences between VME and PCI, and they are especially connected to interrupts. VME has 7 interrupt levels, with a wealth of interrupt vectors[13], while PCI 'only' offers 4 interrupt lines (lines A through D) without the additional mechanism of Interrupt Vectors. The Interrupts are mapped to certain interrupt vectors internally to provide a general system interface. This is a system design. Go check your BSP for specifics if you need to create a driver in this environment!

This results in the effect that we no more have a direct one-on-one connection between the creator of the interrupt and the vector being called. Additionally, there may be several sources connected to the same interrupt line. CompactPCI[14] with its wealth of PCI-to-PCI bridges creates an even more complicated scenario as more and more devices may be connected to a single line.

The way around this is the way VxWorks handles interrupts in architectures which may support PCI, namely PowerPC, SPARC and Intel. Here, not only one but several functions may be connected to an interrupt vector. Every single function then needs to check whether the device is 'responsible' for actually generating the interrupt. If yes, handle the interrupt and **return()**, if no, **return()** without any action.

The disadvantage of this method is that, with only one function, you can disconnect the function from the interrupt if it is no longer needed by connecting the default ISR, telling the user "uninitialized interrupt for interrupt vector XX", to the respective

---

[13]The mechanism of interrupt vectors is based on the MC68000's interrupt handling, being the grandfather of VME and VMEbus!

[14]CompactPCI is an industrial implementation of PCI in the eurocard format – pretty much like VME. This allows for rack-mounted systems with exchangeable cards

interrupt. This is no longer possible when you can connect several functions to the interrupt vector.

You should also be advised that all Interrupt Service Routines for a specific handler will be executed no matter which one of them is "responsible" for the device creating the interrupt. Background of this is that several devices may have pulled the interrupt line at the same time or while the ISR is running.

This means that every ISR should first check whether or not its device has created the interrupt and **return()** if not.

5.8.4 Emergency Interrupts – NMIs

NMIs, short for **N**on **M**askable **I**nterrupts are interrupts of the highest possible level. Their purpose is to enable a system to directly react to events which very deeply affect the system, no matter what action is taking place at this moment. This may be due to a power failure, system failure, watchdog timeout or other events. If something like this happens, you need to directly react to the situation without wasting any additional time. That is the reason for the existence of NMIs.

System Action due to an NMI

Whatever the system may currently be executing, at the moment the NMI arrives, the system starts to execute the NMI interrupt handler, without saving current register set or other necessary information. This may even happen at interrrupt level!

The result is that VxWorks has no provisions to continue working after the occurrence of an NMI. Because it is so urgent to start the handler and react to this scenario!

This means that returning from the NMI may work a thousand times, but it may fail any time! So, ensure your NMI handler ends with the call **sysToMonitor()**, executing a reboot of the system. For everything else, all normal rules for interrupts apply. Only, NMIs are more important interrupts than others, and slightly different...

5.9 Staying Portable

Code which is called portable means that this code can be run on several different platforms. In general, a platform may be an operating system, a certain type of hardware or any combination of both. Due to these demands there is quite a bit of work involved which, however, most likely will pay off. So, let us have a look at this hot issue of today, why it is hot and what is behind it.

5.9.1 Reasoning

Why should you try to use different techniques to stay portable? Direct device programming is a lot faster, and simpler, too! So, why bother with this additional burden?

5.9. STAYING PORTABLE

The answer is quite simple – because you will probably get advantages out of it. Let us take the example of setting an LED to red while explaining the benefits (and shortcomings) of being portable.

First, your code becomes a lot more readable and self-explanatory. A function call to xxSetMyLed(RED) is a lot more readable and clearer for later review than the possible equivalent *(char*)(0xfeff9876) = (char)0x12.

Second, if your platform changes, chances are high that you just will not find your LED in the same place – so, if writing non-portable, you have to do a find/replace across your whole source code, replacing the wrong address with the correct one and verifying you do not replace look-alikes which do something completely different — a difficult task! Otherwise, you only need to change ONE function in ONE location.

Every now and then, you may need to create code to be run on several platforms. Here, probably just a few changes plus a recompile are necessary to make your code run on the new platform. Do you know beforehand whether or not this will be the case?

Downsides? Sure. Encapsulating hardware always means additional function calls which cost time. A way around this is the C++ keyword inline which allows to place function code right in the place of the function call[15]. This may not necessarily remove the complete overhead involved, though.

Another downside is the additional time you need to design your 'hiding library'. But you may save this time sooner than you expect...

An extreme example for extreme portability (and the problems involved) is the GNU project. *gcc* runs on virtually any platform around. Looking at the code shows the effort necessary to achieve this goal.

5.9.2 Considerations for staying Portable

What can you do to really stay portable?
Quite a lot! So let us have a closer look at all these issues.

Standards Conformance

To remain portable, the first of the safe choices is to stay as close as possible to established standards. This means, that you simply adhere to the functions which stem from standard libraries as far as possible. All additional functions will create a need to either re-create them on any other system or major rework to wrap this system's functions in order to make them look like the original system's.

From this point of view, it may be worth the effort to establish a private standard library which then only has to be ported to a new system instead of having to re-port the whole application. This is a frequently used concept, even in operating systems.

---

[15]The downside of inline is that it increases code size. But that is a price to pay for the convenience. Just remember that you need to ensure correct dependencies of your source code files to avoid using two versions of the function declared inline!

92   CHAPTER 5. PROGRAMMING

Additional benefits in this area are reduced debugging time due to major parts of the code already having been tested and debugged before.

On the other hand this area needs some care – different compilers always have different behavior concerning optimization, data packing and other parameters. So, code which works without any problems using one compiler may exhibit totally unexpected behavior when compiled with a different compiler. This takes some testing to be sure everything has been transferred reliably!

The standards conformance will also be discussed a bit further down in this chapter, when talking about POSIX. This is one way of staying portable, but not the only one. Also, you need to make sure that POSIX compliant libraries are available on all or most platforms (if it is not available, it will not be of any help, of course...!).

Hardware Encapsulation

Hardware encapsulation simply means that the thoughts expressed before are used with regard to hardware.

In general practice, this means that you need to create an abstraction layer on top of which the final software will run. This again reduces porting efforts because only this abstraction layer has to be ported.

Some things to keep in mind in this area are data formats (little vs. big endian), processor specifics (e.g. out of order execution etc.) and other behavior. Code running without a flaw on one system may exhibit problems on other systems due to different hardware specifics.

An example would be a PowerPC running in big endian mode, accessing PCI devices. While drivers may work without any problem on Intel processor based systems, the same drivers will probably fail when run on a PowerPC. Why? Because the PowerPC is running in big endian mode, and that means that you need to swap bytes when accessing PCI devices!

Library Approach   To keep these accesses cleanly separated, I would suggest a hardware-dependent file, or directory, which contains the system dependent functions. This also allows for #define dependent inclusion of specific files or functions while offering an obvious separation. Take a look at GNU software which shows a great example of how software can be made hardware specific yet portable. Do not follow everything, as this would probably be quite an overkill, but take it as an example to look at!

Driver Approach   Drivers in general have been discussed in chapter 5.7.1. So you will only find a few remarks on advantages and disadvantages of drivers in general, as seen from a portability point of view.

Device drivers are a generic way of accessing devices through the I/O system. This bears several advantages:

5.9. STAYING PORTABLE

- General Interface, Device Independence

    I/O System drivers all have interfaces to the standard system functions **open()**, **close() read()**, **write()** and **ioctl()**. So, if you need to replace the driver, your application code may stay the same, as long as the device name remains the same.

    And, even that can be overcome using a #defined device name.

- Access Control

    The operating system may offer some facilities for controlling access to devices. If you write a standard driver, you get these additional functions from the O/S for free.

- Additional Facilities

    Additional facilities which can be used by a driver would be additional O/S facilities, like STREAMS, C++ iostreams and others. By writing a driver for the O/S, you get this additional feature without additional effort; additional facilities like support for **select()**, for example, will need to be added to the driver if they are to be used by the application.

Disadvantages are basically performance loss due to being channeled through the I/O system, plus the in comparison fairly inflexible way of handling the device: you need to work through file descriptors, use **read()**, **write()** and **ioctl()**. This may prove fairly cumbersome for some purposes, but offers improved portability and simple replacement of outdated devices – it is your choice!

Additionally, of course, this is a lot more readable and understandable for persons who need to maintain your code. Again, it is your choice whether you want this to happen or not – or someone else's.

Coding Conventions

General information on C(++) Programming Techniques can be found in [Dav93]. What is the deal with them?

Coding Conventions imply a set of definitions of how the code needs to be indented, documented and defined. Additionally, this also defines how functions are to be named and the way they may be called.

Killer-editors like EMACS can be configured to at least perform the indentation and documentation parts of coding conventions automatically or partially automatically. Check your documentation!

A set of definitions like this creates a huge advantage which should be taken into account whatever you intend to do with the code later. So, let us have a closer look:

- Readability

    Code which adheres to a defined convention is a lot more readable than 'homebrewed' code. The background is that this way you know what to expect when you try to find source code for a function. The set of parameters is presented in a specified way, allowing for common understanding and prototyping.

    Also, people tend to read clearly spaced code a lot better than "I only need two lines" code!

- Documentation

    A coding convention normally also defines a way of documenting the created source code. As this means it has to be done in a uniform way, it will be documented automatically. This saves time when reworking the code later.

- Error-Reduction

    A definition of how to handle code reduces the amount of errors when calling functions as well as a proper definition of variable and function names. So, at the end of the day, less time is spent debugging the 'simple' errors!

Enough about generals, now let us have a look at what comes out of the box without having to do additional work.

Object Orientation

What does Object Oriented Programming have to do with portability? At a first look, nothing. Looking a second time, you can gain a lot here. Using a clean design plus inheritance, you can very cleanly encapsulate hardware dependencies and also make sure your code remains very safe all over.

Inheritance allows you to create software which, for common features, uses common code. So, once this code is tested to work properly, it is really safe to re-use it! Anything inheriting this now, will also be based on this, known-to-work, safe code.

General Ways to stay on the Safe Side

Something else which comes with a C++ compiler, without the need of really creating C++ code. C++ implements very strict type checking. Also, *gcc* allows for very strict checking of other variables. So, as a first test before even starting to debug, run *gcc* -pedantic -Wall on your code. This will yield a whole lot of messages, but also help avoid a lot of unfound or (when reusing the code) different errors! Fix these messages as they exist for a reason! At least, they point you to possibly critical operations.

5.9. STAYING PORTABLE

5.9.3 POSIX.x

POSIX (Portable Operating System Interface) is a very general term with many different aspects including User Interface, commands etc. For VxWorks, only some of those aspects are really of interest. As VxWorks uses a host-based programming environment, the POSIX conformance for *that* is to be part of the host operating system. The conformance itself only extends to the programming interfaces.

Especially the real-time extensions of POSIX are covered in the VxWorks POSIX libraries.

For a more general introduction to POSIX Real-time Extensions, see [Gal95]. This book shows most important functions and their meanings down to a very detailed discussion of the different functions and is so very much to be considered as the 'standard' on this issue.

The different POSIX versions and their Meanings – An Overview

POSIX definitions have quite a number of scopes and numbers. The ones of interest plus their implications and effects on VxWorks, will be discussed below.

VxWorks in itself, where applicable, complies to only some of the POSIX versions.

POSIX 1003.1 — Basic O/S Interfaces This is the very basic POSIX standard. It defines the different interfaces to the O/S.

To some extent, this certainly applies to VxWorks. Double-check the manual to really know what is available, and what is not. Where things are available, you should try to stick to the standard.

POSIX 1003.2 — Shells and Commands This defines a basic set of shells and commands to be part of a POSIX compatible operating system. This to some 90 % extends to today's UNIX systems. But not all of them comply to all – look for POSIX compatible signs.

As the Tornado *WindSh* and the target shell are both more or less home-grown C interpreting shells with add-ons, this part certainly does not apply to VxWorks. It may apply to your development platform, but this does not make a difference for software development.

POSIX 1003.3 — Testing Methods Certainly not applicable to the system — maybe to Wind River's methodology... You should certainly have a look at this for your own development and testing.

POSIX 1003.4 — Real-time Extensions This is the area which is really of interest for VxWorks, being a real-time operating system. Here, the basic libraries and functions will be discussed. For more specific information, refer to [WRS99l] and the online documentation.

96   CHAPTER 5. PROGRAMMING

POSIX usually names functions like **clock_gettime()**; library first and then the function name. This helps to tell both POSIX and possibly standard O/S functions apart.

VxWorks POSIX 1003.4 Implementation

In general, the POSIX libraries in VxWorks are implemented as wrapper-functions for the normal built-in calls. This has several effects and caveats.

So, after the general subsection, let us now look at different aspects of the VxWorks implementation.

Clocks and Timers Enabled through #define INCLUDE_POSIX_TIMERS.

In addition to the standard *tickLib.h* defined functions, VxWorks offers support for a POSIX compliant interface to the system's clocks and timers.

There are some facts you should know up front.

The library is implemented as wrapper classes to the standard timer library *tickLib.h*. The result of this implementation is that the minimum timer resolution is limited to $\frac{1}{sysClkRateGet()}$ sec (normally $\frac{1}{60}$ sec) even though there are functions like **microDelay()**, or, for instance, **nanoSleep()** etc., which seem to imply a higher resolution. The timer tick remains the base unit of the system!

The system clock rate is available through **sysClkRateGet()**. It may be set using **sysClkRateSet()** to a user selected rate, but that adds an additional burden to the system due to the added interrupt load. Additionally, in a standard system, the system clock also triggers the scheduler which may or may not be desired. The variable **kerneltimeslice** may help here. However, it also changes the scheduling algorithm, so watch out for side effects.

Beyond that, only the CLOCK_REALTIME is implemented. VxWorks out of the box does not support a possibly available Real Time Clock (RTC). If you need it, you need to create your own library and manually include it.

Anyway, the POSIX library's function names have the prefix **time_XXX()**.

An additional time-related function provided is the **gmtime_r()** function. It allows second to UTC broken-down **struct tm** conversion, as defined in POSIX in a reentrant way.

Asynchronous I/O Enabled by setting #define INCLUDE_POSIX_AIO.

Asynchronous I/O is a way to perform I/O without stopping a task, waiting for instance for the hard disk to finish writing the data. This basically works in a way that the I/O request gets posted and is performed outside of the actual task context. After completion, the task is notified. All included functions follow a mechanism of **aio_XXX()**.

The Asynchronous I/O works in the following way: one or more tasks are run by the system which is responsible to handle all asynchronous I/O requests. A request is

5.9. STAYING PORTABLE

described by an asynchronous I/O control block which also includes a pointer to what needs to be worked through the I/O process. The process then will perform the I/O requested and then, on completion, notify the requesting process of the result.

Intertask Communication and Synchronization Enabled using:

- #define INCLUDE_POSIX_MQ for message queues,
- #define INCLUDE_POSIX_SEM for semaphores and
- #define INCLUDE_POSIX_SIGNALS for signals, respectively.

An additional area that is well covered in VxWorks is the area of intertask communication and synchronization, represented by pipes, named pipes, message queues, semaphores and signals.

Message Queue functions are denoted by the prefix **mq_XXX()**; they simply map to 'normal' VxWorks message queues without mapping them to files as they are in UNIX. Creation is achieved using **mq_open()**, deletion via **mq_unlink()**. Something you should really refrain from doing is to try standard VxWorks functions on POSIX-created message queues and vice versa. The result may but does not need to work!

Semaphores are handled through **sem_XXX()** functions. Again, this is nearly identical to the VxWorks functions, but do not mix them, either!

The same is true for signals. They are two different kinds of beast, even though they look pretty common.

Scheduling Functionality Enabled using #define INCLUDE_POSIX_SCHED.

The **sched_XXX()** functions allow changes to the way the VxWorks Scheduler works and also to the way a specific task is scheduled in terms of yielding the CPU, changing the task's priority etc. Something you should be sure of is that all these functions' priority values depend on the global variable **posixPriorityNumbering**. If this variable is FALSE, the 'normal' VxWorks priorities apply, if it is TRUE, the POSIX values apply. So, the result achieved may be rather different from what was expected...

5.9.4 Conclusion

At the end of the day, what do you get from using POSIX?

Upside: improved portability, more general interfaces.

Downside: additional latency due to the wrapping character. You will hardly see it these days unless your system is really used to the max.

So, it remains your choice. But, not knowing about it being there would really be bad!

Chapter 6

VxWorks Modules

The goal of this chapter is not to provide in-depth information on each of the different additional parts. It will give pointers to where to look for what.

The basic architecture has been discussed in chapter 2, Basic Concepts. This enables a lot of modules which may or may not be taken away – take a look at *target/config/all/configAll.h* at the `#if TRUE` area! Most of the definitions selectable there are described in appendix A, page 139. See there for a more complete description. Here, we will discuss both main modules and their more important parts plus additional background information.

As of Tornado 2.0, life has become a lot easier, especially in this area. Now, by just selecting or deselecting a module, you can directly see the interdependency of all VxWorks modules. But be careful with your own application modules – the Project tool *may not* work there...!

So, let us have a look at the general background first.

6.1 How and Why does adding/removing Modules affect the Kernel Size?

This answer is fairly simple – use an intelligent linker program to take advantage of this! Well, how does it work?

6.1.1 Background – Symbol Tables

When compiling C source code, the compiler creates a symbol table in each single object module. This gives the linker the information it needs to be able to link your codes together and verify that all functions needed are actually available.

Find below the table for our small demo program as used in chapter 5. You can find the source code in appendix B.2, page 161.

```
00000000 b .bss
00000000 d .data
00000000 t .text
00000000 t ___gnu_compiled_c
         U _printf
00000010 T _rtc
         U _taskDelay
00000000 t gcc2_compiled.
```

This output has the following meanings; lower-case characters signal symbols local to the module, upper-case ones which are visible globally. There are the three standard segments: bss, data and text. Then, there are the two hints at gcc and its version (gcc version 2). All these symbols are local, as signified by the lower-case characters. The only symbol visible to the outside world is the C function **rtc()**, with the two externals **printf()** and **taskDelay()**.

See table 6.1 below for a more complete list.

Type	Meaning
A	absolute symbol, global
a	absolute symbol, local
B	bss (uninitialized data space) symbol, global
b	bss (uninitialized data space) symbol, local
D	data object symbol, global
d	data object symbol, local
F	file symbol, global
f	file symbol, local
N	symbol without type (*no* type), global
n	symbol without type (*no* type), local
S	section symbol, global
s	section symbol, local
T	text symbol, global. This is used for functions.
t	text symbol, local
U	undefined symbol, global. This needs to be satisfied by external libraries!
u	undefined symbol, local

Table 6.1: Symbol Types in Object Modules

These symbols are also used to create the symbol table file, *symTbl.c* when compiling the kernel.

6.1.2 Linking the Modules

When linking, the linker reads this symbol table to determine which symbols are delivered by this module, adds them to its internal symbol table and reads which symbols are needed by this module and checks them against its internal symbol table. This also explains why the order of linking may make a difference – if functions which are needed at this point are not included yet, the link may fail.

If all functions delivered by the module are not needed at any point, this module is discarded by the linker to optimize the object code size. This has the advantage that only modules which are needed will be part of the final kernel, but if you do link your application to the kernel but do not call any of its functions, it will be discarded by the linker, too! So, you need to make sure you call at least a setup function initially.

This basic functionality is the reason of how the VxWorks kernel size can be changed by adding and removing modules even though they are all part of the standard system library file.

6.2 Basic Modules

VxWorks comes with a basic set of modules configured into the kernel out of the box. Some of these will be discussed here as an example as well as others which may be of use.

6.2.1 Networking

The networking support is one of the major advantages of VxWorks. Even though the module can be removed, it offers a lot of additional functionality. The kernel's networking abilities out of the box are BSD 4.4 compliant; VxWorks can handle one startup defined gateway as standard setup which is enough to reach the boot host. To use additional routes after that, you simply add them manually using the command **routeAdd()**.

Also, password protected logins are a non-default feature. You need to use #define INCLUDE_SECURITY plus the function **loginUserAdd()** to allow specified logins. Remember there is a default user and password set up in *configAll.h*!

Networking is also used as the basis for debugging via the WDB agent.

Shared Memory Network

The Shared Memory Network simply implements a protocol driver which runs in place of the Ethernet driver. That way it is intended to simply plug-in instead of or beside the original networking driver[1].

---
[1] See also chapter 4.1.5 on page 57 for additional information.

6.2.2 SCSI

SCSI is another method to store data and programs locally. Even though this is very convenient, it is not part of the standard setup simply because of its size and because some boards simply do not feature SCSI interfaces. The definitions in *config.h* are there, though.

How to use and set up SCSI devices, especially if you want to boot from them, can be found in chapter 4.1.4, page 48. The positive information on SCSI is that this is a well documented, industrial strength industry standard.

It is described here because it is more like a built-in functionality which belongs to the basic set of functions compared to additional features which may be desirable but not at all necessary.

6.2.3 Target Agent and Target Shell

There are two basic user interaction modules which are included in the operating system. The first module is the target agent. The setup which is the base for Tornado, needs a network or serial connection between target and host. The footprint on the target system is relatively small, but the load induced by the tight network connection is comparably high. So, go for this module unless you cannot spare network load or the system load created by the network driver.

If you do have a problem in this area, the target based shell certainly is a choice.

6.3 Optional Modules to add Functionality

This chapter show some important additional functions which add many possibilities to the application.

6.3.1 FTP Server

An FTP server needs the network, of course. This enables a data transfer without taking away too much of the target system's performance. To make it work, though, you need to enable security and set up users who will be allowed to login to your system.

A possible application would be something like a data gathering application running on the target, saving its data to a local hard-disk. Then, every few hours, the main server ftps into the target and picks up the new information.

6.3.2 NFS

NFS is a network protocol which allows for a transparent access to file systems on a remote server. As NFS also provides for file locking and partial file access, the file accesses look exactly the way they would look on a local media.

6.3. OPTIONAL MODULES TO ADD FUNCTIONALITY

The big advantage of NFS is that you can access files byte by byte, compared to the standard network driver which loads a file completely into memory before executing any operations on it. In comparison, *netDrv* uses a lot more local resources.

6.3.3 NFS Server

Nearly everything that applies to the FTP server is also true for the NFS service. Additionally, the NFS server allows access without needing a login to the target system.

As this is all freely shared, security issues need to be considered!

6.3.4 Rlogin and Telnet

rlogin and telnet are two UNIX protocols to connect to remote machines. If your target system is connected to a network but is not too dependent on it, while you do not want to impose the network load of running a target server for it on your network, this may be the choice for you.

In principle, this is a way to get direct shell access to your target, allowing you to run whatever program or do whatever is possible from the *target shell*. And *this* is the major point – you need to `#define INCLUDE_SHELL`, plus, maybe, symbol table synchronization etc. for use of this feature. Certainly something to think about...

Also remember to enable security plus a password protection.

6.3.5 SENS

As of Tornado 2, SENS is the standard network stack which brings an all new protocol stack to VxWorks. This stack offers BSD 4.4 features and more, including DNS, DHCP[2], Routing, the Network Time Protocol and several other additions. Make sure there is a driver available for your system, if you are running older versions of VxWorks or using older systems.

In some cases, due to different driver names, you also may want to consider using the BSD drivers as far as they are available. This needs a lot of consideration and is definitely nothing you should do unless you have to. In time, these drivers will die-out anyway!

Consult with your hardware manufacturer and WRS for specifics.

---

[2]Be warned! This DHCP implementation is compliant to RFC, while the MS Windows NT implementation is slightly different! There have been some problems reported.

Chapter 7
Important BSP Information

As the BSP in itself renders a lot of information and configuration possibilities for your system, we had better have a look at what is where and which files are of particular interest.

After that, we will also have an additional look at important general VxWorks files and their functions.

For more information on *make* and tools, also see appendix B, page 159. Also remember the warning about using both IDE and *config.h*, page 32!

7.1 BSP Files

There are several important files which show you many important settings and selections concerning the BSP as well as, in the comments, additional selectable options. So, let us have a look around at some key files. If you need to make serious adjustments, you should definitely make yourself comfortable with the different files and what is where.

Again, the files of the PowerCore BSP will be used as base for the discussion. Here, some parts will be omitted, signified by (. . .).

7.1.1 *Makefile*

The Makefile is the starting point of any kernel compilation. Here, some basic settings like ROM address etc. are made.

```
# Makefile - makefile for bsp/config/pcore604
#
# Copyright 1996-1997 FORCE COMPUTERS GmbH.
#
# modification history
# --------------------
# 02b,19aug97,lsr  Renamed BusNet EXTRA_INCLUDE to BUSNET_INCLUDE
```

This line is important to find out both current version and additional information. It tells you about date and current version, *who* made this change (if you know what the initials stand for...) and what was changed. This is the standard header for *all* BSP files delivered in source.

Basically, this header includes all information needed to create e.g. a *man* page.

```
#
# DESCRIPTION
# This file contains rules for building VxWorks for the
# FORCE COMPUTERS PPC/PowerCore-6750 VME Board.
#
# INCLUDES
#     makeTarget
#*/

CPU             = PPC604
TOOL            = gnu
```

So now, the pre-settings for both toolchain (Usually either Diab Data or GNU gcc tool family) and CPU_TYPE[1] are selected for all sub-Makefiles. Below, some system pre-settings for directories to be used later are defined, before including the next set of general definitions as delivered with the operating system.

```
TGT_DIR=$(WIND_BASE)/target
include $(TGT_DIR)/h/make/defs.bsp
include $(TGT_DIR)/h/make/make.$(CPU)$(TOOL)
include $(TGT_DIR)/h/make/defs.$(WIND_HOST_TYPE)
```

Below, we find BSP specific selections like board type, board vendor etc. which will be compiled into the kernel.

```
## Only redefine make definitions below this point, or your
## definitions will be overwritten by the makefile stubs above.

TARGET_DIR        = pcore6750
VENDOR            = FORCE
BOARD             = PowerCore-6750

EXTRA_DEFINE      = -D_GNU_TOOL -DTARGET_DIR="\"$(TARGET_DIR)\""

RELEASE           = vxWorks vxWorks.st bootrom.hex

USR_ENTRY         = usrInit
```

Now, we need to set up compilation specific values to be used for ROM setup, entry point addresses etc. RAM_LOW_ADRS and RAM_HIGH_ADRS are used for starting the kernel when starting out of flash. One thing to remember: the space in between these

---

[1] for valid values, see appendix A.2, page 157

7.1. BSP FILES

two values should be big enough to allow for the whole kernel. Otherwise, you may encounter unexpected problems when running out of flash.

The hex flag -a 100 is used because, for PowerPCs, the start address has an offset of 0x100 into the flash memory which will be built to begin at 0xfff000000.
After that, a vendor-specific library is linked into the kernel.

```
#
# The constants ROM_TEXT_ADRS, ROM_SIZE, and RAM_HIGH_ADRS are
# defined in config.h, MakeSkel, Makefile, and Makefile.*
# All definitions for these constants must be identical.
#

ROM_TEXT_ADRS    = fff00100    # ROM entry address
ROM_SIZE         = 00040000    # number of bytes of ROM space

RAM_LOW_ADRS     = 00100000    # RAM text/data address
RAM_HIGH_ADRS    = 00200000    # RAM text/data address

HEX_FLAGS        = -a 100

MACH_EXTRA       =

LIB_EXTRA        = $(TGT_DIR)/config/force/lib/lib$(CPU)$(TOOL)frc.a

## Uncomment the 2 following lines for BusNet
#BUSNET_INCLUDE  = -I$(TGT_DIR)/src/config.BusNet
#CONFIG_ALL      = $(TGT_DIR)/config/all.BusNet

EXTRA_INCLUDE    = -I $(TGT_DIR)/config $(BUSNET_INCLUDE)


## Only redefine make definitions above this point, or the expansion
## of makefile target dependencies may be incorrect.

include $(TGT_DIR)/h/make/rules.bsp
include $(TGT_DIR)/h/make/rules.$(WIND_HOST_TYPE)
```

The last two lines are the most important ones. The *make* targets like *vxWorks* or *bootrom* are defined in the file *rules.bsp*.
The host specific definitions are defined in the file *rules.$(WIND_HOST_TYPE)*.

7.1.2 config.h

This file is the command center for the BSP. If the modules to be included are selected in *configAll.h* you will find fine tuning parameters as well as additional settings which influence the BSPs behaviour here. So, for *config.h*, we need a more detailed discussion.

108 CHAPTER 7. IMPORTANT BSP INFORMATION

The file used here is just used as an example of what can be adjusted and selected in *config.h*. So, you need to read your own file very carefully. This serves as an example for what to look for.

```
/*
This file contains the configuration parameters for the
FORCE COMPUTERS PowerCore-6750 VME boards.
*/

#ifndef __INCconfigh
#define __INCconfigh

/* BSP version/revision identification, before configAll.h */
#define BSP_VER_1_1     1
#define BSP_VER_1_2     BSP_VER_1_1
#define BSP_VERSION     "1.2"
#define BSP_REV         "/1-0"  /* 1st release for Tornado 2.0 */
```

Now, the basic definitions for the BSP are set: we have a version 1.2 BSP, subrevision 1. There are several versions for BSPs, 1.0 for pre-Tornado BSPs, 1.1 for Tornado 1.x BSPs and 1.2 for Tornado 2. Below, the pre-settings which need to be in place before including *configAll.h* are set up, then the more general files included.

```
/* SCSI-2 inclusion macro before configAll.h */
#if TRUE
#define INCLUDE_SCSI2
#endif

(... PMC/860 description omitted ...)

#undef FRC_PMC860_WITH_16MB

#include "configAll.h"
#include "pcore750.h"

/* default boot parameter */
#define DEFAULT_BOOT_LINE \
    "frcDec(0,0)host:/usr/tornado/target/config/pcore750/vxWorks"\
    "h=90.0.0.3 e=90.0.0.50 u=target"
```

Above, you find the default bootline which is used if there are no valid NVRAM parameters. As the first location of the NVRAM is only checked for being 0x00 in *bootConfig.c* to determine whether we have a valid bootline or not, this is used very seldomly. If you want to make this check more efficient, you need to modify this file. But, as you are making changes to system files in this case, you really should consider whether you really need it or not – moving to a new version of the O/S will require you to recreate this change!

7.1. BSP FILES

If your target does not supply any NVRAM, this line needs special attention. It needs to mirror set up and the definitions you need. The information will then be used in any case.

LongCall support is crucial for systems running in more than 32 MB of memory. By default, this is not enabled.

Remember? This needs to be enabled and recompiled into all libraries!

```
/*-------------------- PPC specific defines -------------------*/
/*
 * longcall support:
 * if the user application supports the longcall patch to break
 * the 32MByte memory boundary, FRC_SUPPORT_LONGCALL must be
 * defined to configure the BSP.
 *
 * Note: this define does not change any compiler options!
 */
#undef  FRC_SUPPORT_LONGCALL
```

Now, we need to define the NVRAM parameters and the basic information for the serial interfaces.

```
/*----------------- Miscellaneous definitions ------------------*/

/* NVRAM */
#define NV_RAM_SIZE         (BBRAM_SIZE - 0x08)   /* 1k reserved */
#define NV_RAM_ADRS         ((char *)BBRAM_ADRS)
#undef  NV_BOOT_OFFSET
#define NV_BOOT_OFFSET      0

/* serial interface */
#undef  NUM_TTY
#define NUM_TTY             (sysNbUart())
/*
 * The 16550 serial devices supports FIFO for the receive and
 * send of characters. In this mode the device generates fewer
 * interrupts(only after a certain amount of characters). Per
 * default the BSP initialize the devices in this mode, undefine
 * the following macro to get the device to run in a character
 * based mode (1 interrupt per character transmitted or received).
 */
#define SIO_FIFO_ENABLE

(...)
```

Definitions for a FORCE COMPUTERS specific PMC module removed.

```
/* defines for PCI writes */
#define PCI_WRITE_LONG    sysWordSwapWr
#define PCI_READ_LONG     sysWordSwapRd
```

110   CHAPTER 7. IMPORTANT BSP INFORMATION

This way, we make sure that the PCI definitions work correctly.
Below, memory and cache are configured.

```
/*-------------- Memory, Cache and MMU configuration -------------*/
/* Cache configuration */
#define USER_D_CACHE_ENABLE       /* enable data cache */
#define USER_I_CACHE_ENABLE       /* enable instruction cache */

#undef  USER_D_CACHE_MODE
#define USER_D_CACHE_MODE         (CACHE_COPYBACK | CACHE_SNOOP_ENABLE)
```

MMU full mode would mean that we are using VxVMI. As this is an optional add-on package, the definition should not be touched.

```
/* MMU configuration */
#undef  INCLUDE_MMU_FULL
#define INCLUDE_MMU_BASIC         /* Bundled mmu support. */
```

Now follows the SCSI configuration. As already shown in chapter 4.1.4, this allows for some configuration. The config is way down in the config file and will be discussed down there.

```
/* -------------- SCSI configuration ----------------------*/
/* If the board contains a SCSI PMC module or SSIO SCSI can */
/* be enabled. */

#undef  INCLUDE_SCSI_PMC
#undef  INCLUDE_SCSI_SSIO
```

Flash support is a FORCE add-on. So, we will skip this part.

```
/*-------------------- flash memory support -------------------*/
#define INCLUDE_FLASH             /* include flash memory support */

(...)
```

Timer definitions follow. If you are using WindView, you may want to #define INCLUDE_TIMESTAMP. This will enable timestamping the different events. Additional information here: the CIO timer is used for the auxiliary clock, additionally, we are defining max and min rates for the clocks. *Do not change these values!* Even though we are in *config.h*, this does not necessarily mean we can edit everything. Some things simply should be treated as informational only.
More timer settings are defined far below.

```
/*----------------- configure the needed timers ----------------*/
/* Include for WindView support */
#undef  INCLUDE_TIMESTAMP         /* include timestamp timer */
```

7.1. BSP FILES

```
#define INCLUDE_Z8536_AUXCLK    /* use CIO timer for auxClock */
#undef  INCLUDE_Z8536_CLK       /* use PPC dec timer for main clock */

/* CIO timer */
#define ZCIO_CNTRL_ADRS         ((volatile UINT8 *)(Z8536_PORT_CTRL))
#define ZCIO_HZ                 (Z8536_SPEED_HZ / 2)
#define ZERO                    0
#define ZCIO_RESET_DELAY        5000

#define AUX_CLK_RATE_MIN        32   /* Minimum auxiliary clock. */
#define AUX_CLK_RATE_MAX        5000 /* Maximum auxiliary clock. */
```

Now, we can make some changes as well as get some information. Below, the slave addresses are set up, dependent on **sysProcNumGet()** to allow for non-overlapping VME slave regions even with several boards running the same kernel. This is of course only true if you set the processor number to a different value...

As visible here, there is no access to the local memory from A16 VME address space.

At the bottom, there are definitions for Write Posting, i.e. decoupling the actual access from the actual data transmission (the VME master gets a DTACK before the actual write transaction is completed).

This has the advantage that the transaction is completed very fast. The disadvantage is, that, whenever the access fails, the master still is left under the impression of having transmitted data correctly, while it actually has not. While developing, this should better not be enabled, for the production system, where speed is more important, this should be considered for performance reasons. Remember, though, that this may cause problems due to built-in timing restraints to your application!

```
/*----------------------- VMEBus defines -------------------------*/

/* base address of the Universe */
#define UNIVERSE_BASE_ADRS      ((sysProcNumGet() << 12) & 0x0000f000)

/* VME Slave Interface */
#define VME_A16_SLV_SIZE    0
#define VME_A16_SLV_BUS     0
#define VME_A16_SLV_LOCAL   0
#define VME_A24_SLV_SIZE    0x00100000
#define VME_A24_SLV_BUS     (sysProcNumGet()*0x00100000)
#define VME_A24_SLV_LOCAL   0
#define VME_A32_SLV_SIZE    LOCAL_MEM_SIZE
#define VME_A32_SLV_BUS     ((sysProcNumGet()*0x04000000)+0x20000000)
#define VME_A32_SLV_LOCAL   0

#define VME_SLAVE_WPOST_EN        /* Enable/Disable write posting */
#define VME_SLAVE_PREFETCH_EN     /* Enable/Disable read prefetch */
```

CHAPTER 7. IMPORTANT BSP INFORMATION

Below, we find the definitions for the master accesses to VME. The local addresses are defined in *pcore60x.h*, while the bus addresses (i.e. window *to* VME lower border) can be configured. Whenever you want to access an address which is outside this window, your access will fail!

The definitions below will be used in the functions **sysLocalToBusAdrs()** and **sysBusToLocalAdrs()**. To have transparent access plus safe, portable access to defined regions, always use these commands when initializing!

This has already been discussed before, see page 75, chapter 5.6.1!

```
/* VME Master Interface */
#define VME_A16_MSTR_SIZE      0x10000
#define VME_A16_MSTR_BUS       0x0000
#define VME_A16_MSTR_LOCAL     PCI_IO_VME_A16
#define VME_A24_MSTR_SIZE      0x1000000
#define VME_A24_MSTR_BUS       0x000000
#define VME_A24_MSTR_LOCAL     PCI_MEM_VME_A24
#define VME_A32_MSTR_SIZE      0x30000000
#define VME_A32_MSTR_BUS       0x20000000
#define VME_A32_MSTR_LOCAL     PCI_MEM_VME_A32
```

Again, the remarks on Write Posting from page 111 apply, this time seen from the master side. So, for development, disable and for deployment, enable!

```
/*
 * Please read the UNIVERSE User Manual and Errata Sheets
 * before enabling write posting!
 */
#undef VME_MASTER_A32_WPOST_EN  /* En-/Disable A32 write posting */
#undef VME_MASTER_A24_WPOST_EN  /* En-/Disable A24 write posting */
#undef VME_MASTER_A16_WPOST_EN  /* En-/Disable A16 write posting */
```

Here, we are now pre-setting the VME options. Arbiter settings are only valid if the machine is slot 1 device. This is also true for the bus timeouts. One thing to remember is that this is board specific — some may have these settings in hardware! The definitions may look different for other boards, too.

```
/* VME Requester and Arbiter configuration */
#define VME_ARBITER_MODE       MISC_CTL_VARB_PRI
#define VME_ARBITER_TIMEOUT    MISC_CTL_VARBTO_16U
#define VME_BUS_TIMEOUT        MISC_CTL_VBTO_64U
#define VME_RELEASE_MODE       MAST_CTL_VREL_RWD
#define VME_REQUEST_LEVEL      MAST_CTL_VRL(3)
#define VME_REQUEST_FAIR
```

DMA functions are built-in special functions for FORCE, so we will skip this part.

```
/* This section includes the defines for the VMEbus DMA. */
#undef INCLUDE_VME_DMA
(...)
```

7.1. BSP FILES

The next part defines settings for the network interfaces. ENP and EX are old, VMEbus card-based interfaces. For backward compatibility, they are still available.

SM_NET is the standard backplane network protocol as delivered with VxWorks. By #undefining it here, you can gain some space here. Remember that this steals a network-like communications means from your system.

BusNet it a FORCE developed cross-O/S replacement for this driver, the FRC_DEC is a FORCE-specific branch of the standard DEC 21140 driver. .

```
/*-------------- configure the network interfaces ---------------*/

/* SENS - Extended Network Driver support */
/* (only applicable if SENS has been installed) */

#if TRUE       /* select either END or BSD 4.4 style driver */
/* select (define) or unselect (undef) enhanced network drivers */

#define INCLUDE_END    /* Enhanced Network Driver see configNet.h */

/*
 * Select (define) END_OVERRIDE to enable an END ethernet interface
 * after booting via a non-END ethernet interface.
 */
#define END_OVERRIDE   /* define if you are using old boot ROMs. */

#else

#define INCLUDE_BSD    /* BSD 4.4 style driver */

#endif

/* exclude unused network device drivers */
#undef   INCLUDE_ENP
#undef   INCLUDE_EX

/* define the backplane network interface */
#define  INCLUDE_SM_NET
#undef   INCLUDE_BUSNET

/*
 * include DEC Chip 2114x driver
 * (must also be defined if using the END driver)
 */
#define INCLUDE_FRC_DEC

/*
 * define this to use the backplane (aui) connector instead of the
 * front (tp) connector. (SENS/END driver only!)
 */
#undef PCORE_CNFG_END_AUI
```

CHAPTER 7. IMPORTANT BSP INFORMATION

Next in the config file are the base definitions to set up the Shared Memory Network. Normally, the only parameters to edit are SM_TAS_TYPE and SM_MODE, depending on your system. The major fact to keep in mind is not to mix the TAS[2] modes.

This is a crucial issue. If one of the boards can not execute an atomic TAS cycle, you *must* use Software TAS. What is that?

Software TAS emulates the behavior of Hardware TAS. That means:

- The CPU which executes the TAS reads the corresponding location.

- If it is non-zero, the TAS fails and returns.

- If it is zero, a value is written to the location.

- To verify no one else stole the lock, the location is polled 10 times. If the value changes within this time, the lock was stolen and the TAS fails.

- If the location remains the same, the TAS succeeds.

What is the tradeoff here?

Well, the behavior is well-emulated. But, there are some possible issues here that need to be taken into account.

Imagine one very fast and one very slow board. The very fast one may be done polling before the slow board even finishes writing its footprint to the tested location!

And, polling a location regularly for eleven times plus writing simply is very slow! Plus you have the additional overhead for the explicit compare operations.

So, the software TAS certainly is something to consider, but do not expect world record breaking performance from this technology!

Something else to know about is the notification method, here called SM_MODE. This defines how the board receiving a packet is notified about the arriving packet so it can pick it up. There are three different modes possible:

- SM_POLL is the basic mode. It means that the respective board polls the notification location in the master's memory regularly to find out whether or not a new packet has arrived. This takes most bus bandwidth but works for all types of boards. Especially if crossing busses other than VME, this is a viable choice.

- SM_IT uses interrupts for notification. Due to a limited number of interrupts, this limits the possibilities but is a lot better from a load-perspective than Polling Mode.

---

[2]TAS is short for Test And Set, an atomic VMEbus and 68k instruction which allows to test a location for its value being zero and set it if this is true. Another term for this is Read-Modify-Write, RMW.

7.1. BSP FILES

- SM_MBOX if available, this is the mode of choice. The mailbox accesses mean just one short bus transaction for notification, no interrupt handling outside the board accessed and no additional overhead. However, it mainly applies to VME (some PCI bridges offer similar capabilities today) and may be of limited use.

BusNet definitions omitted here.

```
/*--------------- Backplane network parameters -----------------*/

/* PPC does not support Hard TAS across the VMEBus */
#undef   SM_TAS_TYPE
#define  SM_TAS_TYPE    SM_TAS_HARD

/* Set the backplane mode to be used for shared memory network */
#define SM_MODE        SM_POLL     /* backplane mode, valid are : */
                                   /* SM_POLL, SM_IT, SM_MBOX */

/* Set shared memory driver to use on- or offboard memory */
#define SM_OFF_BOARD    FALSE
```

The memory definitions are vital for setting up the system. Today, autoconfiguring setups are usual, so you do not need to have different kernels for different memory sizes.

But, some users like to be able to do their own configuration. For them, additional manual memory configuration is possible.

Let us look at the following.

The first step consists of misc settings for memory: whether or not memory should be cleared on startup (warning — things tend to take longer then!!) and whether or not ECC should be enabled.

USER_RESERVED_MEM is memory at the top of memory which may be set aside for user purposes. This may be an idea if you need buffers at a fixed address, for instance.

RAM_LOW_ADRS and RAM_HIGH_ADRS are the addresses used for the ROM boot. RAM_HIGH_ADRS is where the system is copied and started to unpack the compressed kernel, RAM_LOW_ADRS is the target where the real kernel code is copied after unpacking. If the space between these two is too small, the kernel will fail to start. Keep this in mind when changing modules or adding huge modules to the kernel.

```
/*---------------------- Memory defines ----------------------*/

/* Memory configuration */
#undef  ENABLE_ECC          /* ECC may only be used on */
                            /* MPC106 REV > 3.0 */

/*
 * This define is used to activate the auto sizing of memory.
 * Additional memory will be dynamically added in sysHwInit.
```

CHAPTER 7. IMPORTANT BSP INFORMATION

```
*/
#define LOCAL_MEM_AUTOSIZE

#define USER_RESERVED_MEM       0x00000000      /* no user memory */
                                                /* reserved */

#define LOCAL_MEM_LOCAL_ADRS 0x00000000         /* Fixed at zero. */

/*
 * CLEAR_MEMORY: clear the memory beyond 32 Mbytes.
 */
#undef  CLEAR_MEMORY

/* LOCAL_MEM_SIZE defines the minimum of the Board's memory */
/*                                        (EDO 16 MB). */

#define LOCAL_MEM_SIZE          0x01000000      /* 16 Mb minimum */
                                                /* board memory */

#define RAM_LOW_ADRS            0x00100000
#define RAM_HIGH_ADRS           0x00200000      /* RAM address */
                                                /* for ROM boot */

/* flash memory defines */
#define BOOT_FLASH_SIZE         0x00080000 /* 512k Boot flash size */
#define USER_FLASH_SIZE         0x00400000 /* 4M Userflash size */

/*
 * The constants ROM_TEXT_ADRS, ROM_SIZE, RAM_LOW_ADRS and
 * RAM_HIGH_ADRS are defined in config.h, MakeSkel and Makefile.
 * All definitions for these constants must be identical!
 */
#define ROM_BASE_ADRS           0xfff00000
#define ROM_TEXT_ADRS           (ROM_BASE_ADRS + 0x100)
#define ROM_SIZE                0x00080000      /* 512k ROM space. */
```

The final three constants above are used for romming the system and the bootrom. They determine the major parameters when starting the system from ROM and should only be changed if you know what you are doing. Additionally, as the comment above states, you also need to set these parameters in the *Makefile*.

Below this place, the specific definitions for the different functions and settings follow.

First, there is the possibility for you to add another reconfiguration file that will be included here automatically by defining OTHER_CONFIG_FILE for the compilation.

```
/* --- Include additional (re)configuration file if any --- */

#ifdef OTHER_CONFIG_FILE
#include OTHER_CONFIG_FILE
#endif
```

7.1. BSP FILES

The next lines define the cache configuration.

```
/*------------ Memory, Cache and MMU configuration ---------------*/
/* enable of L2 cache is only useful if L1 cache is enabled */
#if defined (USER_D_CACHE_ENABLE) || defined (USER_I_CACHE_ENABLE)
#define L2_CACHE_ENABLE        /* enable L2 cache */
#undef  L2_CACHE_COPY_BACK     /* enable L2 in copy back mode */
#undef  L2_CACHE_DATA_ONLY     /* L2 data cache only */
#endif
```

If we have set up a SCSI PMC module, no automatic configuration is used (as already discussed above, we have created our own SCSI configuration function!) and then the DOS FS is used.

```
/*------------------- SCSI configuration -----------------------*/
#if     defined(INCLUDE_SCSI_PMC) || defined(INCLUDE_SCSI_SSIO)
#undef  SCSI_AUTO_CONFIG   /* SCSI auto configuration */
#define INCLUDE_SCSI       /* include scsi driver */
#undef  INCLUDE_SCSI_BOOT  /* include ability to boot from SCSI */
#define INCLUDE_DOSFS      /* file system to be used */
#endif  /* INCLUDE_SCSI_PMC */
```

The next lines set up the timer definitions. Note that the min and max values are hardware parameters and must not be changed.

```
/*----------------- configure the needed timers -----------------*/
/* timestamp from Z8536 can only be used in conjunction with
 *  main clock */

#if     defined(INCLUDE_TIMESTAMP) && defined(INCLUDE_Z8536_CLK)
#define INCLUDE_Z8536_TIMESTAMP
#endif

/* Maximum and Minimum Clock Rates */
#ifdef INCLUDE_Z8536_CLK
/* Min and Max value for the Z8536 Timer */
#define SYS_CLK_RATE_MIN   32   /* Minimum system clock rate. */
#define SYS_CLK_RATE_MAX   5000 /* Maximum system clock rate. */
#else
/* Min and Max value for the PPC decrementer timer */
#define SYS_CLK_RATE_MIN   10   /* Minimum system clock rate. */
#define SYS_CLK_RATE_MAX   5000 /* Maximum system clock rate. */
#endif
```

Here, there are register settings for the network interface. Just ignore them...

```
/*---- define parameters for DEC 2114x network device driver ----*/
#if defined(INCLUDE_FRC_DEC) && !defined(INCLUDE_END)
#define PCORE_DC143_REG_VALUES { 0, 0, 1, 0, 0, 0, 0x1, \
                                 0x20, 0, 1, DEC_MII};
```

118 CHAPTER 7. IMPORTANT BSP INFORMATION

```
/*
 * The following defines are used for selection of either the AUI
 * (in SSIO) or MII port for the ethernet connection. Due to using
 * a standard driver automatic selection is not possible. To use
 * the front panel Ethernet (MII) connection use the frcDec or
 * frcDec0 interface. To use the backplane Ethernet connection (in
 * SSIO) use the frcDecB one.
 */

#define NETIF_USR_ENTRIES \
    { "frcDec",  sysFrcDecattach, (char*)NULL, PCORE_DEC_MII }, \
    { "frcDecB", sysFrcDecattach, (char*)NULL, PCORE_DEC_AUI },
#endif   /* INCLUDE_FRC_DC && !INCLUDE_END*/
```

BusNet parameters ignored.

The Shared Memory Network parameter settings here are as usual set to on-board SM network. When should you use off-board Shared Memory? This was intended for memory cards somewhere in the system to be used as data exchange area. Today, this is mainly obsolete and not needed any more.

Note that the Tundra Universe I (outdated) offers an interrupt bit which may be used to generate a mailbox interrupt as set up below; the Universe II offers standard mailboxes.

```
/*---------------- Backplane network parameters -----------------*/
#if     SM_OFF_BOARD
#undef  SM_ANCHOR_ADRS
#define SM_ANCHOR_ADRS   ((char *)0xa0000000)
                                /* off-board anchor address */
#define SM_MEM_ADRS      SM_ANCHOR_ADRS
                                /* off-board S.M. adrs. */
#define SM_MEM_SIZE      0x00040000
                                /* shared memory pool 256K */
#define SM_OBJ_MEM_ADRS  (SM_MEM_ADRS+SM_MEM_SIZE)
                                /* SM Objects pool adrs */
#define SM_OBJ_MEM_SIZE  0x40000
                                /* SM Objects pool size 256k */
#else
#define SM_MEM_ADRS      0x00010000  /* NONE = allocate from mem */
#define SM_MEM_SIZE      0x00040000  /* shared memory pool 256K */
#define SM_OBJ_MEM_ADRS  0x00050000  /* SM Objects pool adrs */
#define SM_OBJ_MEM_SIZE  0x00040000  /* SM Objects pool size 256K */
#endif   /* SM_OFF_BOARD */

/* Polling */
#if     SM_MODE == SM_POLL
#define SM_INT_TYPE      SM_INT_NONE       /* polling */
#define SM_INT_ARG1      0                 /* unused */
#define SM_INT_ARG2      0                 /* unused */
#define SM_INT_ARG3      0                 /* unused */
```

7.1. BSP FILES

```
#endif    /* SM_MODE==SM_POLL */

/* Use VMEBus interrupts */
#if       SM_MODE == SM_IT
#define SM_INT_TYPE     (SM_INT_BUS)            /* bus interrupt */
#define SM_INT_ARG1     (sysProcNumGet() + 1)   /* level */
#define SM_INT_ARG2     (0x40)                  /* vector */
#define SM_INT_ARG3     0                       /* unused */
#endif    /* SM_MODE == SM_IT */

#if       SM_MODE == SM_MBOX
#define SM_INT_TYPE     (SM_INT_MAILBOX_1)      /* mailbox */
#define SM_INT_ARG1     (VME_AM_SUP_SHORT_IO)   /* bus addr space */
#define SM_INT_ARG2     ((UNIVERSE_BASE_ADRS) + 0x0348)
                                                /* bus address */
#define SM_INT_ARG3     (0x01)                  /* any value */
#endif    /* SM_MODE == SM_MBOX */
```

This implements warning messages for the ECC and CLEAR memory settings that need some pre-requisites.

```
/*----------------------- Memory defines -----------------------*/
/* CLEAR_MEMORY: takes effect only if LOCAL_MEM_AUTOSIZE is defined.*/
#if       (!defined (LOCAL_MEM_AUTOSIZE) && defined (CLEAR_MEMORY))
#warning CLEAR_MEMORY takes effect only with LOCAL_MEM_AUTOSIZE enabled !
#endif

/*
 * ENABLE_ECC should only be used if CLEAR_MEMORY is defined.
 * Otherwise it will generate ECC errors if accessing the no
 * clear/initialized memory area (upper than LOCAL_MEM_SIZE)
 */

#if       (!defined (CLEAR_MEMORY) && defined (ENABLE_ECC))
#warning  ENABLE_ECC should only be used if CLEAR_MEMORY is defined !
#endif
```

This is the final but most important line. If the configuration using the project facility (as is usual today) is used, include file here.

```
#if defined(PRJ_BUILD)
#include "prjParams.h"
#endif
```

7.1.3 <BSP_NAME>.h

This file contains all board specific definitions. So, if you need to program a board's hardware, you should both #include this file and also have a close look at the definitions here.

They set up the general parameters for the board, addresses for chips, I/O and other important addresses. If you do low level programming, this is the place to start.

7.1.4 sysSerial.c

This file contains the initialization of the serial interfaces. Have a look at which chips are used and how they are setup here as well as which adjustments can be made using **ioctl()**.

7.1.5 sysScsi.c

This file — present only for boards that actually have a SCSI interface — is one of two places to look for SCSI setup specifics. This file contains the board specific SCSI initialization functions plus additional setup routines. The application specific initialization of the different devices connected to the SCSI bus is done in *...target/src/config/usrScsi.c*. The functions there are called if `SYS_SCSI_CONFIG` is defined. See chapter 4.1.4, page 48 for more information on SCSI boot and SCSI configuration.

7.1.6 sysVme.c

This file also only exists for VME boards. It is the place to look for VME specific setups. Here, slave and master windows are setup together with some additional definitions. As the basic settings are done in *config.h*, you normally should need to use this file for reference only. But you never know, so better have a look here as well.

7.1.7 sysLib.c

This library contains the board specific functions which are defined in a general way for VxWorks like **sysBusToLocalAdrs()** etc. As these functions are board specific, they need to be part of the BSP. If you need information on what one of these functions does, look here first; but you normally should only use this file as a reference, not as a configurable part of the BSP. Here, also the different hardware setups and chip initializations can be referenced. So, this file is certainly a wealth of information for those who like to read C code...

Important Functions

There are several functions in *sysLib.c* the user should pay special attention to. They are either specific to the respective board's hardware, and, normally, give a lot of information on the hardware setup.

- **sysLocalToBusAdrs()**

  This is the address translation function for VME. It is used to determine where on VME for a given Address Modifier a local address will be visible.

7.1. BSP FILES

If this function returns **ERROR**, the address given is not accessible, either due to the Address Modifier or to the address not having been mapped. See chapter 5.6.1 on VME windows, page 75 for more information.

Warning! When manually programming the bus bridge hardware without updating this function, the values returned will probably be incorrect!

- **sysBusToLocalAdrs()**

  This is the counterpart function to **sysLocalToBusAdrs()**, telling you which local address you need to access to access the given address using the given Address Modifier. Again, **ERROR** is returned if there is no way to reach the address; also, the statement on manually changing the hardware setup applies.

- **sysProcNumSet()**

  This function is not just used to specify the Processor Number[3]. It is also used for several additional actions. Check the BSP source code to see what is happening to you here!

  For example, in some 68k BSPs, the slave window is only enabled for processor number 0; and that is done in this function.

- **sysProcNumGet()**

  The counterpart to **sysProcNumSet()**, without the additional implications.

- **sysHwInit()**

  This function contains the first steps of the BSP hardware initialization. If you need to know how your hardware is set up, have a first look here.

- **sysHwInit2()**

  The second step when initializing the system.

- **sysHwInitOem()**

  OEM specific initialization function. This may or may not be present, depending on the way your hardware vendor has set up the BSP.

- **sysHwInit2Oem()**

  Second step when setting up the system. The same as stated above is true here.

---

[3] see also chapter 4.1.1 for more information on the boot parameters

7.2 VxWorks System Files

These are files as delivered with Tornado/VxWorks. As there are also several implications in these files which may or may not be agreed on by the user, we will discuss their most important parts.

One remark to be made up front: whenever touching files in the main configuration directory .../target/config/all, remember that these files are generic for *all BSPs*. Also remember to create a backup. If something goes wrong here, you will have a very bad time getting back to a working solution if you do not have a backup. There is hardly any way to debug the bootrom!

7.2.1 bootConfig.c

As .../target/config/all/bootConfig.c consists of more than 1000 lines of code, we will only discuss its most important functions.

bootConfig.c is the file executed in the bootrom. So, this file contains the basic bootprom code, the most important initialization functions to enable the board to come up (i.e. callouts to the different BSP functions) plus some interesting user-configurable settings.

7.2.2 usrConfig.c

.../target/config/all/usrConfig.c is *bootConfig.c*'s equivalent for the kernel when coming up.

It contains a bit more, though. This "C" source code file #includes several other system startup files, placed in other directories of the VxWorks installation, e.g. .../target/src/config/usrNetwork.c.

7.2.3 usrScsi.c, usrIde.c

.../target/config/<Your_BSP>/usrScsi.c contains the board specific initialization of eventual SCSI interfaces. Here, some setups can be modified to fit the application. Something similar is true for *usrIde.c* that holds similar information for IDE based systems.

7.2.4 usrNetwork.c

.../target/src/config/usrNetwork.c executes the actual network interface initialization. It should be used for reference only and normally does not provide any additional useful information.

7.2.5 usrApplInit.c

The file .../target/src/config/usrApplInit.c defines the function **usrApplInit()** that can be used to start your application code from **tRootTask**.

7.3 Gathering Additional Information

In the installation tree, there is a lot of additional information available in the *man* pages as delivered with the UNIX system. Some older BSPs do not come with Windows .HLP files, so you may need to get the man command from a GNU server.

In addition, you may want to format and print man pages. How to do that, was shown at the very beginning of the book on page 21.

Chapter 8

Tailoring Your Setup to Your Needs

This is one of the main tasks in general application development. Tornado comes which some additional tools that may help here and are discussed below as well as general concepts of what can and what cannot be done.

Whatever you do using Tornado-based tools, keep in mind they may need a network connection to your host system! This may have some impact on your system's behavior. The effort is very application dependent; you should know about it and keep it in mind — just in case!

The following steps will be reviewed below:

- Clean up the kernel to leave only the modules needed
- Review the optimization level of your application
- Profile your application to find areas for improvement
- Use WindView to find critical sections
- Tailor your application for best performance and safety

Now, let us have a look at what can be done...

8.1 Cleaning Up the Kernel Modules

In order to make your final application fit into whatever resources you have available, it may be necessary to strip away all unnecessary kernel facilities you used throughout development. There are many things to think about. Some are listed here:

- Do you need a target resident symbol table?

    The symbol table will only be necessary if you are adding functions by downloading additional code or if you want to be able to access your system manually from a local shell or via the network.

126   CHAPTER 8. TAILORING YOUR SETUP TO YOUR NEEDS

- Do you need a target based shell?

  If there are problems on your target system, this may come in handy if you want to do a few tests. But, you will also need to have the symbol table available - otherwise you will not be able to access any functions...

- Do you need networking?

  If your final system is not connected to a network, and never will be, why add the overhead of having a network stack on your system? This also takes away some space in your memory and ROM.

- Do you need specific networking services?

  Other services which are included by default are FTP Server, NFS, Telnet, Rlogin etc. If you do not need them, you should get rid of them.

- Do you need the Wind Debug Agent?

  The Wind Debug Agent will only be necessary if you expect to continue using the Tornado tools. If this is not intended, you should remove it as well. Just to get more space on your target system.

- Finally remember to disable debug information on your final rebuild!

As of Tornado 2.0, this task has become a lot less tedious. Using the Project tool, you can configure your system to basically run bare-bones with only the parts included which are really needed, thanks to its ability to know the interdependence of the different system modules.

Nevertheless, a bit of knowledge may help up front to prevent using features that may result in direct inclusion of very big additional modules.

One of the biggest modules necessary and used is networking. If you do not need networking, you can get rid of a lot of space used in system memory or ROM.

Just remember: Fewer functions, less overhead, less to execute.

8.2 Optimization

Compilers allow for general optimization settings, see appendix C on page 165. Though the options are very general *(-O[01236])*, this of course offers the easiest way of improving performance.

But one warning here: using a specific optimization level (the higher the more dangerous) also makes some assumptions on the code. They may or may not be correct, causing the compiler possibly to make optimizations which are invalid under different circumstances.

To stay on the safe side one should review the different optimization options one-by-one and then choose specific optimization options. This takes a lot of time and

8.2. OPTIMIZATION

thought, so it will only be a viable way for much-used, critical modules. The more modules you have, the more specific you can choose your options. Normally, after profiling the code, you should review your modules and choose which ones should, after using a general optimization level of -*O1*, be optimized using a higher optimization level.

The results of -*O2* already become difficult and should be tested carefully; -*O3* and, especially, -*O6* are to be tested very thoroughly before being released. In any case, an assembly code review might prove very helpful here!

A safer way for the optimization would be a per-module definition of specific optimizations. For a complete list, dependent on the processor-architecture, see the GCC manual.

Some common pitfalls regarding optimization: the compiler will make assumptions on your goals and what you want to do. The following, very common spinlock should illustrate this:

```
int lock10(char *here)  /* lock location, test 10 times */
{
    int i;

    if (*here != 0)   /* cannot lock - someone else has got it */
        return ERROR;

    *here=0x10   /* set lock */

    for (i=0; i<19; i++)
        {
            if (*here != 0x10)   /* lock stolen! */
                return ERROR;
        }

    return OK;
}
```

Optimization will make this function look as follows:

```
int lock10(char *here)  /* lock location, test 10 times */
{
    int i;

    if (*here != 0)   /* cannot lock - someone else has got it */
        return ERROR;

    *here=0x10   /* set lock */

    return OK;
}
```

If you are really lucky, you may even retain the **for()**, but nothing more!

CHAPTER 8. TAILORING YOUR SETUP TO YOUR NEEDS

What happened?

Very simple. The compiler does not know that the location given here may be changed from the outside. So, it assumes that the only access to this particular location can come from the program itself, which does not make this access. So, remove the test because without it, it is faster!

How do you make sure this does not happen? There are two alternatives.

One is to tell the compiler to assume all variables as **volatile**, i.e. can be changed without the compiler knowing about it. This means that it will not optimize any access, thus yielding very slow code. But, nothing like the example above can happen. The option to use would be -fvolatile.

The best way is to tell the compiler explicitly that *this* particular variable may be subject to outside change by using the designator **volatile**. So, the code above should read:

```
int lock10(volatile char *here)   /* lock location, test 10 times */
{
  int i;

  if (*here != 0)   /* cannot lock - someone else has got it */
     return ERROR;

  *here=0x10   /* set lock */

  for (i=0; i<19; i++)
    {
       if (*here != 0x10)   /* lock stolen! */
          return ERROR;
    }

  return OK;
}
```

A simple change, but with huge implications.

8.3 Profiling

What is profiling? Profiling is a method to find out which parts of the software actually are used, and how much time has been used in the respective function. This allows you to direct your optimization efforts to where they will be most efficient.

It may be used on a module- and function level basis. While the function level is *very* detailed, it is usually too detailed for general analysis. So, start on a module basis to see where time is being spent and then move to a more detailed view of those modules where most time is spent.

For profiling, there is no built-in method in VxWorks. But, there are third-party tools which allow you to do profiling-like tasks.

8.3.1 RTIlib – A Utility Library

RTIlib actually comes with StethoScope and is an additional library which allows lots of utility calls PLUS a profiler.

8.3.2 Coverage Analysis Tools

The additional tool CodeTest which was originally intended to perform code coverage analysis, also allows profiling the source code, finding which parts of the code are executed and the timings of them.

With the information from this tool, you can find which part of the code really should be looked at closely for optimization, and which will not be really useful because it is only executed once. Now, as you know what to optimize, you may e.g. want to re-order your statements and function flow to allow for faster execution.

As an additional benefit, you can prove how much of your code was tested throughout your testing cycle. Quite a few customers and managers will absolutely love this!

8.4 WindView to Enhance System Performance

WindView adds the ability to run a logic analyzer in terms of viewing which task is run when, and which events lead to which reaction. This can be used to find bottlenecks, race conditions and other problems which are usually not found using standard debug techniques.

The major first step to decide if you want to use WindView is instrumentation.

8.4.1 Instrumentation

Instrumentation means that you can add events WindView will register to your application. Doing that, you can see when these points are met, what events happen before and after, and what special steps can be taken.

This allows several issues to be cleared. The following sections give more information on what that may or may not mean.

- Identifying Race Conditions

    WindView allows you to see where two tasks are competing for one resource where each one keeps the other from gaining access and finishing in an orderly fashion.

- Finding Bottlenecks

    Find the application tasks and parts that are executed very often, and start optimization here! This is where you get the most benefit out of your efforts!

130   CHAPTER 8. TAILORING YOUR SETUP TO YOUR NEEDS

- Finding where the application crashes

  This is a kind of abuse of WindView, but one in which WindView is very valuable: you can save a snapshot of the events when the system fails and afterwards analyze what happened en route to the crash. But, because you will need to instrument the area where things happen in a very detailed manner, this is nothing to do for the final application.

  It steals both time and performance...!

8.4.2 Modes

WindView has two different modes. Depending on what you need to do, choose the appropriate mode.

Life Mode

This is the simplest and most convenient mode. It is nice to watch your system while it is running (which may be very interesting to find many possible reasons of failure), this comes at the cost of additional network bandwidth used for the data transfer plus some internal loss due to increased interrupt and network stack load!

Post Mortem Mode

This is the most tedious but a very valuable mode: it will tell you what happened in the last seconds your system was still alive. So, you can see that the IRQ on level 5 all of a sudden caused task 13 to run instead of the usual 1-2-3 behavior... And you can see where to look for the set of circumstances that made your system fail!

Again, this is just a start for finding causes, but if everything else fails (which is very common in today's multitasking, complex systems), this is where you can get the additional hints you might need!

8.4.3 Limitations

You should always remember that everything comes at a price. Whenever you run WindView or enable WindView, this means a degradation in performance, due to the instrumentation being run under many circumstances. Adding WindView Instrumentation to your application also means some additional load, both for your application execution time and memory being used. As always, there is a tradeoff.

If you run WindView in Life Mode, you also add a lot of network load in addition to your normal load. This may or may not impact your system. If resources are scarce, it may even lead to failure of your system!

Whereas this performance loss is lower in Post Mortem Mode, this mode means loss of memory.

8.5. TAILORING THE SYSTEM TO YOUR APPLICATION

Also just remember that you can only see what you make visible! Just starting WindView may tell you many things, but you can only see detailed information the moment you add reasonable instrumentation to your application!

8.4.4 Things To Do After Using WindView

Finally, for your final application build, you should remove WindView from the Tornado set up to make sure you do not get the additional overhead for the instrumentation. You should also have your application constructed in a way that it will disable your instrumentation the moment you compile without #define INCLUDE_WINDVIEW! Otherwise, you might not only have to pay a huge penalty in terms of additional memory needed but you will also see undefined references...!

At the very end, make sure that, by removing WindView, you did not speed up your system and make it fail due to implicit time dependencies (that might also make it fail when moving to a new processor but remain invisible with WindView included), i.e. make sure you do extensive testing after the removal.

8.5 Tailoring the System to your Application

So now here we are, we know all we need to know below our application level to make the system you are designing upon meet the needs of your application.

This chapter is set up as a kind of checklist of what you should do, what you should look at and other things that should be considered.

8.5.1 Application Structure

Let us have a look at what your application should do, and how. The cleanest way is to look at common structures and separate them from the bulk of the application. So, fixing one problem means it actually is fixed for all uses in your application.

One of the main good ideas at this point is to make a drawing of the different structures in your application.

Distributed Structure

The distributed structure is meant in two ways. One is to really look at the local distribution of your application – what is done where?

If you have several processing units involved, create a drawing showing which tasks need to be achieved by them. Additionally, look at what logical code parts may be shared here. Maybe, you only need to create and recompile a special, common library for all target systems.

This means less to maintain, which is critical for quick, safe development.

So, tear your application apart – what do you need on host 1, what on host 2 etc. Look at tasks and basic functions for these tasks!

Dependencies and Connections

Look at what you need where. What information needs to be available where, and how is it passed on?

What protocols are necessary, do you need to create your own protocol? If you do, create (and really draw) your own statemachine and make sure you do not loose any error states or possibility of what can go wrong (a "misc error" message may work wonders here...).

Look at your different states, the different possibilities of error messages coming in. Define the error messages you want to pass on to your user and make them human-readable. Possibly, you also want to add your own error messages to the definitions of Wind River's messages. If so, see chapter 3.1.1, page 25, for more information!

8.5.2 Hardware Setup

This subsection is about what to look at in the hardware you expect to use. Which special functions do you need — did the hardware manufacturer (or whoever wrote the BSP!) cater for what you need?

If not, look around for the information you need to accomplish your goals. Have a look at the manuals, memory maps and chip manuals. Find out whether there are other drivers available you may want to use — Linux is a good choice here due to freely available drivers, at least for standard devices!

Now, find out how you need to set up the hardware in use, maybe even create a model for the chip. Also, create structures (or classes) to be in a good position for writing readable code controlling the device.

Available Hardware

Depending on the interfaces you intend to use, have a closer look at the hardware. Possibly the manufacturer already delivers sample code for VxWorks or other, competitor's operating systems which will allow a simple initialization or port.

Something else you may want to look at might be Wind River's Device Drivers CDROM. It delivers quite some ready-to-use drivers. So, why invent the wheel twice?

Another good place to look is Linux. There are lots of ready-made drivers waiting for you to port them out there.

Anyway, many things need to be done up front. See below...

8.5. TAILORING THE SYSTEM TO YOUR APPLICATION

Memory Map

So now here we are. We know which devices to use, how to program them and we already have done the preparational stuff. Now, look at the next topic: the memory map.

Why is that so difficult today? Well, in the times of VME, addresses were fairly fixed or at least prepared by the BSP manufacturers. This is no longer true with CompactPCI. Here, the host processor should map all cards in the system to appropriate addresses. And, to do so, *you* need to invest some time and thought into what needs to be mapped where! Also, you may need to check what your BIOS did in case of using a PC-like architecture.

To do so, prepare a list first, showing all devices you need mapped which are not mapped by the BSP up front (if they are, note what is mapped where, and which resources are used up), and which resources they use (memory space, I/O space). Now, distribute them according to your needs and create a first header file mirroring your needs in its definitions.

Interrupt Map

Many devices also will use one or more interrupts. Just do the same as above for the interrupts, create another set of definitions for these. Make sure the right interrupt service routines get connected to the right interrupts. Again, add your definitions to your custom header file.

8.5.3 System Design

That is it. Now, from a system perspective, you can create your code. Right? Wrong! What you can do now is...

- Create a System startup function to download, initialize and start your application code.

- Create the drivers you need for your application.

- Modify the BSP to add the memory mappings you need for your application.

Now, the basis is set up.

So, there is some code to be created. But, the major part of the application is yours to define and decide upon. That is the software architecture you intend to run with.

Software Architecture

This small section intends not to take away the work you need to do to create your application but just to ask a few questions you may want to consider and give a few hints of what you may want to look at while finalizing your application.

Task and Interaction Model When creating a multitasking system, you should always keep in mind the interaction between tasks, and how they work together. If passing messages or working with events, keep in mind that someone needs to wait for the events and needs to handle them.

To make sure there are no loose ends left, draw a picture detailing the interaction and make sure all messages and events are included. Then, check against your application code.

Drivers or Libraries This is one of the major questions. Libraries are easier to write and more difficult to maintain. they are nicer and better tailored to your exact needs but normally not portable at all. So, your checklist could look as follows:

- Will I need this software on other platforms?
- What about two years from now? Still the same platform? Sure?
- Will this platform be supported by the hardware manufacturer over a longer time? Is there a contract in place to ensure this?
- Any projects in sight where the code may be re-used?
- Will the software be a one-time-shot?

If more than one of these questions is answered towards a driver, you should go for a driver. You can of course devise your own driver model which not necessarily mirrors Wind River's. But, define a clean interface to keep portability as you will probably need it!

O/S Services – Needed and Unnecessary Ones Look through the kernel as you have been using it throughout development. What will you still need in production? Will you need WDB? Will there be a need for networking? Additional features that are nice while developing may not be desired in the final application. Not everyone should be able to log into your system in the production environment!

But keep in mind – what will you need when things go wrong? A 'syslog' logging facility is nice to have to reconstruct what happened when the system crashed. "Out of Memory" will help a lot to find the culprit.

Finally, these are just a few things to think about when finally putting together your final application. Anyway, make sure to run extensive tests after setting up the final system. You would not be the first in for a surprise that xyz was necessary even though you did not think it was needed!

Chapter 9

Troubleshooting VxWorks

Throughout this book there are many hints about troubleshooting VxWorks. This chapter focuses on pointing back to them and categorizing them properly in order to make trouble shooting easier.

So, browse around for your problem and see whether there are hints on how to resolve it or find the reason for it!

9.1 Installation

Sometimes, things do not work out as smoothly as expected. Especially for older BSPs in current installations, or using the old pre-Tornado2-script *installOption*.

installOption **Troubleshooting.** See page 27.

Items to remember when touching files in *.../target/config/all***.** See page 122.

9.2 Boot Process

Many troubles in VxWorks result from not getting the system to boot properly. Cryptic error messages or no messages at all are pretty common due to the early time of the system startup with no real error handling in place yet.

9.2.1 Shared Memory Network

Slave Window not opened for processor numbers other than 0. See page 42.

SM Anchor not found in memory space. See page 42.

9.2.2 Download Issues

Error message downloading the kernel. See page 45.

No download, no packets on the network. See page 44.

Kernel download using TFTP works OK, but the symbol table download fails. See page 45

Software TAS possible issues. See page 114.

File download fails – out of memory. See page 147.

9.2.3 General Networking Issues

Now, have a more generic look at where things go wrong with the network.

Host name mismatches between network names and names used on the target. See page 43.

After booting the target, other hosts are inaccessible. see page 44.

Many other network boot issues on a page. See page 60.

Downloading code fails with undefined externals. See page 65.

Default username for login to target system. See page 69.

9.3 Running the Target

Here, we also find common issues coming up. Let us have a look...

9.3.1 License Issues

On a regular basis, License issues occur. Suddenly, the license manager does not recognize the license any more, etc. etc.. What can be done?

License file not found.LM_LICENSE_PATH not set See page 36.

9.3. RUNNING THE TARGET

9.3.2 Other Topics while Developing or Running the Target System

Debugging techniques. See page 66.

Typical problems using a startup script. See page 71.

Other reasons for missing or unreachable functions when downloading code. See page 72

Finding out whether a bus location is reachable or not. See page 75.

Trouble shooting device programming. See page 79.

What you should not do with Interrupts. See page 89.

PCI Interrupt Specifics. See page 89.

Why you should never return from NMIs. See page 90.

Compiler optimization possible issues. See page 126.

Common compiler pitfalls. See page 163.

Issues due to cache coherency. See page 141.

Appendix A

Important Defines and Modules

This appendix is intended to provide additional information on several important aspects of VxWorks and add some background information on the modules delivered plus CPU types supported as of today.

A.1 VxWorks Modules

This section presents a comprehensive list of most VxWorks includable modules, what they can be used for and whether or not they may be needed. Additional optional and backward-compatibility modules are discussed as well.

Not all of these options or macros may be available through the Configuration Tool. They can only be accessed by editing *configAll.h* or *config.h* directly. Again, the warning above on page 32 does apply!

As of Tornado II, use of the Project Tool to change the configuration may be a good idea. Anyway, knowing about the background will help a lot if you need to make manual adjustments. Note that there are two different ways of including the modules. If using the Project Tool, *.../target/config/all/configAll.h* will be ignored!

The description shows the group title, a description plus comments on whether this is *default*, *default disabled* or a separate *add-on* to the system, followed by list of the possible definitions and modules.

The Programmer's Guide also has some more information on some of the different packages.

A.1.1 Compatibility Packages

VxWorks is not *that* new. So, as development moved on, some older features were discarded. For compatibility reasons, there is still access available to them if you definitely need it.

Otherwise, stay away from the older modules. Normally, you do not gain anything because there is already something new to replace them. This is all true for the Vx-

Works 5.0 packages. They really only should be used in the very unlikely case that there is no other way to port your application or keep your environment.

The INCLUDE_CONFIGURATION_5_2 definition is different. This will make your system look and feel like the pre-Tornado version 5.2. In some cases, this may be a desirable effect, e.g. having direct serial access to your target using the target based shell and symbol table. So, this is an option to bear in mind!

The older "bp" backplane network driver has been made obsolete and removed as of Tornado 2. It has been replaced by the better Shared Memory Network.

```
INCLUDE_ANSI_5_0     /* include only version 5.0 ANSI support */
INCLUDE_DELETE_5_0 /* define delete() function as in VxWorks 5.0 */

INCLUDE_CONFIGURATION_5_2 /* pre-tornado tools */
```

A.1.2   ANSI C support – default

ANSI C is a standard module which, by default, is enabled completely. If you find you need space and do not use some special ANSI C parts, you can opt to discard parts of it. But you had better be very careful in this area.

```
INCLUDE_ANSI_ALL     /* includes complete ANSI C library functions */

INCLUDE_ANSI_ASSERT      /* ANSI-C assert library functionality */
INCLUDE_ANSI_CTYPE       /* ANSI-C ctype library functionality */
INCLUDE_ANSI_LOCALE      /* ANSI-C locale library functionality */
INCLUDE_ANSI_MATH        /* ANSI-C math library functionality */
INCLUDE_ANSI_STDIO       /* ANSI-C stdio library functionality */
INCLUDE_ANSI_STDLIB      /* ANSI-C stdlib library functionality */
INCLUDE_ANSI_STRING      /* ANSI-C string library functionality */
INCLUDE_ANSI_TIME        /* ANSI-C time library functionality */
```

A.1.3   BootP support – default

BootP is a protocol, which, being a predecessor of DHCP, allowed a system to obtain an IP address plus, optionally, a boot file from a host system somewhere on the network.

This is mostly used by the bootrom; so that a possible rebuild of it may prove necessary when disabling this feature.

```
INCLUDE_BOOTP            /* bootp */
```

A.1.4   BSD socket support – default

Sockets are a common form of communicating in a network system. This is the packet that enables this communication. Beware that there may be other packets implicitly relying on the availability of sockets!

Also, backward compatibility to the older O/S versions is enabled.

A.1. VXWORKS MODULES

```
#ifdef INCLUDE_BSD_SOCKET
  /*
   * By default, set the sockets API for compatibility with BSD 4.3
   * applications.
   */
#define BSD43_COMPATIBLE
```

A.1.5 Cache Support – default

Do not disable this! Modern processor architectures rely on cache memory for their performance. And, even though there may not be chips on the main board, there still may be internal caches inside the CPU module. This is definitely a way to slow down your system very efficiently.

There are however options set in the BSP file *config.h* which affect the cache settings. So, in general, check *that* file instead to enable or disable caches.

Disabling caches in general may be used to find problems with DMA or dual-ported RAM which are created by problems with cache-coherency or drivers which are not written cleanly.

```
INCLUDE_CACHE_SUPPORT       /* include cache support package */
```

A.1.6 C++ support – default disabled

As of Tornado 1.0, full C++-support is part of the standard distribution. As of Tornado 1.01, IOSTREAMS have been added.

```
INCLUDE_CPLUS_MIN           /* include minimal C++ support */
```

is available only prior to Tornado 2 and is obsolete.
Instead, Tornado 2 now offers STL support.

```
INCLUDE_CPLUS               /* include C++ support */
INCLUDE_CPLUS_IOSTREAMS     /* include iostreams classes */
INCLUDE_CPLUS_STL           /* include Standard Template Library core */
```

A.1.7 Wind Foundation Classes – add-on

Additional C++ tools are the Wind Foundation Classes. They consist of a set of VxWorks Wrapper Classes, plus a *tools.h++* implementation for VxWorks. Booch and heap classes were included in the Tornado 1 versions for the Booch [Boo95] and other object oriented development methods. They were not accepted by the users and were removed.

Prior to Tornado 2, the options are as follows:

142   APPENDIX A. IMPORTANT DEFINES AND MODULES

```
INCLUDE_CPLUS_BOOCH      /* include Booch Components library */
INCLUDE_CPLUS_HEAP       /* include Heap class library */
INCLUDE_CPLUS_TOOLS      /* include Tools class library */
INCLUDE_CPLUS_VXW        /* include VxWorks wrapper classes */
```
As of Tornado 2, the options are:
```
INCLUDE_CPLUS_VXW        /* include VxWorks wrapper classes */
INCLUDE_CPLUS_TOOLS      /* include Tools class library */
INCLUDE_CPLUS_STRING     /* include string class */
INCLUDE_CPLUS_STRING_IO  /* include i/o for string class */
INCLUDE_CPLUS_COMPLEX    /* include complex number class */
INCLUDE_CPLUS_COMPLEX_IO /* include i/o for complex number class */
INCLUDE_CPLUS_IOSTREAMS_FULL /* include all of iostreams */
```
The VxWorks wrapper classes are described in [WRS99b].

A.1.8   CodeTest Utility Library — add-on

CodeTest allows debug and coverage analysis of your code. This is an additional tool.

```
INCLUDE_CODETEST         /* CodeTEST target utilities library */
```

A.1.9   Pre-Tornado Debug Facilities – default disabled

This allows the use of the old, remote-debug facility, also called *rdb*. Today, this is replaced by the WDB and its superior abilities. So, this will only be used in an environment which does not provide support for the current version or inter-communication with the older-generation tools.

```
INCLUDE_DEBUG            /* pre-tornado debugging */
```

A.1.10   The DEMO application – default disabled

This application inclusion shows how to start an application from startup while the shell is disabled. The application is very simple; all the code is visible and can be edited in the file *.../target/config/all/usrConfig.c*, the original call is in **usrInit()**. As of Tornado 2, this also needs **usrApplInit()** from *usrApplInit.c*.

```
INCLUDE_DEMO             /* include simple demo instead of shell */
```

A.1.11   File systems – default disabled

Several file systems are supported by VxWorks. This is useful only when working with local devices like RAMdisk, floppy disks or SCSI hard disks. See [WRS99k] for a full discussion of the different file systems.

Tornado 2 has added the Target Server File System to allow access to the host file system from the target through the target server. See [WRS99c] for a complete overview.

A.1. VXWORKS MODULES

143

```
INCLUDE_RAWFS              /* rawFs file system */
INCLUDE_RT11FS             /* rt11Fs file system */
INCLUDE_DOSFS              /* dosFs file system */
INCLUDE_WDB_TSFS           /* target-server file system */
INCLUDE_TSFS_BOOT          /* Boot using Target Server File System */
INCLUDE_TSFS_BOOT_VIO_CONSOLE /* use tgtsvr Console for TSFS_BOOT */
```

A.1.12 Additional Network Interfaces – default disabled

These definitions are available in the *configAll.h* file but should not be used. Normally, definitions of this type should be made in and be part of *config.h*.

```
INCLUDE_ENP                /* include CMC Ethernet interface*/
INCLUDE_LN                 /* include AMD LANCE interface */
INCLUDE_LNSGI              /* include AMD LANCE interface for SGI VIP10 */
INCLUDE_MED                /* include Matrix network interface*/
INCLUDE_NIC                /* include National NIC interface */
```

A.1.13 UNIX-compatible Environment Variables – default

This enables easier porting of UNIX applications by allowing for the usage of environment variables.

```
INCLUDE_ENV_VARS           /* unix compatible environment variables */
```

A.1.14 Basic Exception Handling – default

VxWorks exception handling is routed through a task, tExcTask, which allows for minimum time being spent in exception context and so allowing for a big exception rate. This facility should not be touched at all.

```
INCLUDE_EXC_HANDLING       /* include basic exception handling */
INCLUDE_EXC_TASK           /* miscellaneous support task */
```

A.1.15 Floating Point and *GCC* Floating Point Libraries – default

By default, VxWorks includes Floating Point Libraries; as the compiler tool chain is based on *gcc*, also normally the *gcc* libraries are included. If you want to get rid of them, #undefine these two symbols, but be warned! These are the most commonly found undefined externals in user code!

```
INCLUDE_FLOATING_POINT     /* floating point I/O */
INCLUDE_GCC_FP             /* gcc floating point support libraries */
```

A.1.16 Formatted I/O – default

The ability to do formatted I/O is pretty important; **logMsg()** and **printf()** are based on it, for example.

So, only discard this if you really, really need the space and do not use it at all. Otherwise, better look for other ways to strip down your application!

```
INCLUDE_FORMATTED_IO    /* formatted I/O */
```

A.1.17 FTP Server – default disabled

The standard setup contains an FTP server. This means that you can transfer data from the local data storage (e.g. RAMdisk or SCSI driver) to a client over the network. If you do not need this ability, this is one of the first choices to discard!

If you want to use the FTP server to be able to log into the system, a user has to have a valid user name and a valid password. This is achieved using the SECURITY package plus the command **loginUserAdd()** to add valid users.

```
INCLUDE_FTP_SERVER      /* ftp server */
```

A.1.18 WindView – add-on

WindView is an optional package which allows a graphical display of events, task switches and interrupts by adding instrumentation to the different kernel functions. Additionally, an instrumentation by the user can be added to define user-specific events.

As of Tornado, WindView also uses the *wdb* facility to connect to the target system.

```
INCLUDE_INSTRUMENTATION /* WindView instrumentation */
INCLUDE_WINDVIEW        /* WindView command server */

WV_MODE        CONTINUOUS_MODE
```

See chapter 8.4, page 129, for more information on how to use WindView, the different modes and benefits.

Tornado 2 adds more possible paths to upload WindView data to the host and slightly different WindView setup. The older INCLUDE_INSTRUMENTATION and WV_MODE definitions have been made obsolete.

```
INCLUDE_WINDVIEW           /* WindView target facilities */
INCLUDE_WVUPLOAD_ALL       /* include all Windview upload-path types*/
INCLUDE_WVUPLOAD_FILE      /* include file Windview upload-path */
INCLUDE_WVUPLOAD_SOCK      /* include socket Windview upload-path */
INCLUDE_WVUPLOAD_TSFSSOCK  /* include tsfs sock WV upload-path */
```

A.1. VXWORKS MODULES

A.1.19 The I/O System – default

The I/O system is one of the big pluses of VxWorks. You should only disable this if you absolutely do not make use of the I/O system. This should be one of the very last choices of all!

```
INCLUDE_IO_SYSTEM        /* include I/O system */
```

A.1.20 The Object Module Loader – default disabled

The Object Module Loader is one of the old, VxWorks 5.2 style parts of VxWorks. If you want to log into your target system and then be able to download code, you should enable this feature. If you still want to be able to take advantage of the Tornado tools, you should keep in mind that this additionally yields a symbol table on the target system which needs to be synchronized with the target server's symbol table!

```
INCLUDE_LOADER           /* object module loading */
```

A.1.21 Logging Facilities – default

The logging facility is a big help within VxWorks which allows you to generate output from interrupt level by calling **logMsg()**, which queues the output to a task.

So, this should find itself near the end of your list of discardable modules. Also, VxWorks itself makes some use of this facility.

```
INCLUDE_LOGGING          /* logTask logging facility */
```

A.1.22 Full Featured Memory Manager – default

This is a standard setup for VxWorks. As an option, you might buy third-party memory managers or write your own.

```
INCLUDE_MEM_MGR_FULL     /* full featured memory manager */
```

A.1.23 MIB 2 Support – default disabled

MIB 2 adds another level of networking support to VxWorks by adding SNMP capabilities to your target system. Several sub-options allow selective setup of what is necessary and what not.

```
INCLUDE_MIB2_ALL         /* All of MIB 2 */
INCLUDE_MIB2_AT          /* the AT group */
INCLUDE_MIB2_ICMP        /* the ICMP group */
INCLUDE_MIB2_IF          /* the interfaces group */
INCLUDE_MIB2_IP          /* the IP group */
INCLUDE_MIB2_SYSTEM      /* the system group */
INCLUDE_MIB2_TCP         /* the TCP group */
INCLUDE_MIB2_UDP         /* the UDP group */
```

A.1.24 MMU support Levels - default and add-on

VxWorks MMU support is static by default, i.e. the system MMU is setup at boot time and remains that way until reboot. Memory protection is not enabled by default either. In most cases, this is enough. In some cases, for the sake of the system, additional capabilities to setup the MMU at run time, or to protect certain memory areas are necessary.

These additional capabilities are delivered by the add-on package VxVMI. It is enabled using INCLUDE_MMU_FULL, and then adds not only several functions to manipulate the MMU at run-time but also the additional standard protection of the vector table and the whole text segment.

```
INCLUDE_MMU_BASIC          /* bundled mmu support */
INCLUDE_MMU_FULL           /* unbundled mmu support */
INCLUDE_PROTECT_TEXT       /* text segment write prot. (unbundled) */
INCLUDE_PROTECT_VEC_TABLE  /* vector table write prot. (unbundled)*/
```

A.1.25 Message Queues – default

Message queues are one of the basic building blocks of the system. Again, something at the very bottom of the 'discard' list!

```
INCLUDE_MSG_Q              /* include message queues */
```

A.1.26 Networking – default

Networking support is a very important part of vxWorks. In some cases, as shown in chapter 3.4 on page 38, the included networking is not initialized or is done so by additional definitions. So, normally, this should remain in the system. If it proves unnecessary, though, you win quite a bit of space by discarding the modules!

As usual, **xxShow()** functions cost space but are very convenient while debugging! Keep in mind that these functions output to *stdout*!

To be able to verify network connection etc., a simple utility function called **ping()** has proven very helpful. If you have any doubt whether you can reach a host or not, or about the throughput of your network, include this function!

```
INCLUDE_NETWORK            /* network subsystem code */
INCLUDE_NET_INIT           /* network subsystem initialization */
```

Disabled since Tornado 2:

```
INCLUDE_NET_SHOW           /* network info and status facilities */
INCLUDE_NET_SYM_TBL        /* load symbol table from network */
INCLUDE_PING               /* ping() utility */
```

A.1. VXWORKS MODULES

Additional capabilities since Tornado 2 — default enabled

Due to the new, BSD 4.4 based network subsystem, quite a few new options have been introduced that allow enabling/disabling.

```
INCLUDE_BSD_SOCKET      /* include the BSD socket library */
INCLUDE_ICMP            /* include icmp code */
INCLUDE_IGMP            /* include igmp code */
INCLUDE_UDP             /* include udp code */
INCLUDE_TCP             /* include tcp code */
INCLUDE_NET_REM_IO      /* network remote file i/o driver */
```

Additional capabilities since Tornado 2 — default disabled

some not-so-common features of the IP stack have remained disabled:

```
INCLUDE_ARP             /* user interface to ARP table */
INCLUDE_BSD             /* netif driver support */
INCLUDE_DHCPC           /* DHCP client */
INCLUDE_DHCPS           /* DHCP server */
INCLUDE_DHCPR           /* DHCP relay agent */
INCLUDE_DNS_DEBUG       /* DNS resolver debug mode */
INCLUDE_DNS_RESOLVER    /* DNS resolver */
INCLUDE_IP_FILTER       /* IP filter library */
INCLUDE_FTPD_SECURITY   /* password security for ftp sessions */
INCLUDE_HTTP            /* http server (Wind Web Server) */
INCLUDE_MCAST_ROUTING   /* include multicast routing in the code */
```

A.1.27 NFS Support Packages – default disabled

NFS is the UNIX de-facto standard for accessing remote file systems. There are two stages:

- Being able to access remote file systems, i.e. being a NFS client.

    This has several advantages. As the standard VxWorks network driver uses the FTP protocol to access files, the files get downloaded to the target when **open**()ed, manipulated in local memory and saved back when **close**()ed. Depending on the file size, this may yield a very high memory usage. NFS changes this because only that portion of the file which is needed gets downloaded.

    Additionally, this also solves some problems when downloading big object modules, because they also need twice the space in local memory.

- Being able to give others access to local file systems

    This means that you do not always have to transfer your data yourself, but that e.g. your control computer might get its data itself. This is called being a NFS server.

When being a NFS client, you additionally have the possibility of either mounting all file systems your boot host exports by default or manually. This is selected using NFS_MOUNT_ALL or not.

```
INCLUDE_NFS                 /* nfs package */
INCLUDE_NFS_MOUNT_ALL /* automatically mount all NFS file systems */
INCLUDE_NFS_SERVER          /* nfs server */
```

A.1.28 Pipes – default

Pipes are another means of interprocess-communication which is very common in UNIX systems. This is the way to enable these means of communications in your system.

```
INCLUDE_PIPES               /* pipe driver */
```

A.1.29 POSIX Support - default disabled

As shown in Chapter 5.9.3 on page 95, POSIX is a very convenient way of creating portable software. VxWorks offers several possibilities and levels of support which may or may not be enabled.

```
INCLUDE_POSIX_AIO           /* POSIX async I/O support */
INCLUDE_POSIX_AIO_SYSDRV/* POSIX async I/O system driver */
INCLUDE_POSIX_ALL           /* include all available POSIX functions */
INCLUDE_POSIX_FTRUNC        /* POSIX ftruncate routine */
INCLUDE_POSIX_MEM           /* POSIX memory locking */
INCLUDE_POSIX_MQ            /* POSIX message queue support */
INCLUDE_POSIX_SCHED         /* POSIX scheduling */
INCLUDE_POSIX_SEM           /* POSIX semaphores */
INCLUDE_POSIX_SIGNALS       /* POSIX queued signals */
INCLUDE_POSIX_TIMERS        /* POSIX timers */
```

A.1.30 Remote Serial Connections - PPP – default disabled

PPP is a means of connecting to your target system via a serial line which still offers networking capabilities.

```
INCLUDE_PPP                 /* include Point-to-Point Procotol */
```

A.1.31 PROXY networks – default disabled

The headline is not exactly correct. By default, the client side of the PROXY ARP package is enabled, but the server side is not.

Any way, let us start at the beginning, what is a PROXY ARP network? This network is used to save IP addresses. So, all systems in a subnetwork connect to their

A.1. VXWORKS MODULES

host through a Master CPU. the only address visible outside this subnetworks is the Master CPU's which itself manages the internal connections to the outside.
A full description is located in [WRS99g].

```
INCLUDE_PROXY_CLIENT        /* proxy arp client (Slave Board) */
INCLUDE_PROXY_DEFAULT_ADDR  /* Use eth. addr to generate bp addrs */
INCLUDE_PROXY_SERVER        /* proxy arp server (Master Board) */
```

A.1.32 RAMdrv, A RAM disk driver – default disabled

This driver enables not only virtual disk drives based on local memory, even though this is the original thought behind it. Because it allows for the fact that a pointer to the data area may be used in the setup, it also allows for devices like (static) flash disks as boot devices etc. So, this is a really versatile tool with many uses.

The driver definitely needs to be used together with a file system, see chapter A.1.11, page 142.

```
INCLUDE_RAMDRV              /* ram disk driver */
```

A.1.33 Remote Debugging – default disabled

This is the old, remote debug package, leftover from pre-Tornado times. As this does not deliver any additional functionality compared to WDB, it should simply be disregarded.

When using IMPLEMENTATION_5_2, no debugger is included. This is a way to add debugging back when you do not want to use wdb. Then connect to your target from the debugger and run the function **demo()** using the commands

```
<crosswind> target vxworks <mytarget>
<crosswind> run demo
```

For further and more detailed information, see [FSF99a], the GDB Manual.
This feature has been discontinued as of Tornado 2.

```
INCLUDE_RDB                 /* remote debugging package */
```

A.1.34 rlogin, allowing network access to your target – default disabled

This option additionally needs the target shell and symbol table included, otherwise you will not be able to call any functions. It enables the direct, network based access to your target with the possibility of doing all you need directly on the target system.

windsh offers similar functionality and does not need to keep the symbol table on the target. On the other hand, *rlogin* redirects **stdin**, **stdout** and **stderr** to the network connection.

```
INCLUDE_RLOGIN              /* remote login */
```

A.1.35 Remote Procedure Calls, RPC – default disabled

RPC is a standard UNIX mechanism to remotely execute functions on network hosts. This allows to distribute functions over the network.

```
INCLUDE_RPC                /* rpc package */
```

A.1.36 Shell Security Package – default disabled

This package allows you to secure the target based shell against unauthorized login, similar to the way UNIX protects unauthorized access using passwords.

Another similarity is the reservation of targets in the launcher. The advantage here, though, is that you do not need a steady network connection to keep in touch with the target server running on the network host.

```
INCLUDE_SECURITY           /* shell security for network access */
```

Also note that *configAll.h* defines a default user and password:

```
/* Login security initial user name and password.
 * Use vxencrypt on host to find encrypted password.
 * Default password provided here is "password".
 */

#ifdef INCLUDE_SECURITY
LOGIN_USER_NAME          "target"
LOGIN_PASSWORD           "bReb99RRed"       /* "password" */
#endif   /* INCLUDE_SECURITY */
```

A.1.37 Socket Select() package – default

select() allows to wait for several file descriptors at the same time. This allows for easier porting of UNIX source code.

You should look at this as something you do not want to throw away. Better just to keep it in.

```
INCLUDE_SELECT             /* select() facility */
```

A.1.38 Different Semaphores – default

Semaphores, as the usual means of task synchronization, are used widely within the different programs. Probably, they are used in more places than you expect! So, discard these modules only if you really do not have any other choice.

```
INCLUDE_SEM_BINARY         /* include binary semaphores */
INCLUDE_SEM_COUNTING       /* include counting semaphores */
INCLUDE_SEM_MUTEX          /* include mutex semaphores */
```

A.1. VXWORKS MODULES

A.1.39 Target based shell – default disabled

Another pre-Tornado tool. If you need startup scripts, *rlogin* or *telnet*, this package must be included as well as the symbol table. Otherwise, it should not be.

```
INCLUDE_SHELL            /* interactive c-expression interpreter */
```

A.1.40 Show Routines – default disabled

These functions are very helpful if you need in-depth information on a lot of system facilities or for debugging purposes. So, while debugging, enable this feature, and for production, disable only if you really do not have the space.

```
INCLUDE_SHOW_ROUTINES    /* show routines for system facilities*/
```

A.1.41 Signal facility – default

The signals package allows interprocess communication as well as UNIX compatibility for easier porting.

```
INCLUDE_SIGNALS          /* software signal library */
```

A.1.42 Serial Line IP Package – default disabled

Communication over serial lines today happens usually using PPP instead of SLIP. So, only go for SLIP if you absolutely have to. SLIP is outdated due to its overhead.

```
INCLUDE_SLIP             /* include serial line interface */
```

A.1.43 Shared Memory Network, Communication via a backplane bus – default

The Shared Memory Network allows a network-like communication via a backplane bus like VME or (in the future) PCI. Additionally, this package adds the basic functionality for VxMP, discussed in the paragraph below.

The principles of this network have been discussed already in [WRS99h] and, partially, in chapter 4.

The Sequential Address setup allows for automatic IP address selection, depending on the *processor number*, starting with processor number 0's IP address.

```
INCLUDE_SM_NET           /* include backplane net interface */
INCLUDE_SM_SEQ_ADDR      /* SM network auto address setup */
```

A.1.44 Shared Memory Objects, VxMP – add-on

VxMP offers a communication between different processors which, to the software, looks nearly like normal interprocess communication, running on a single processor.

```
INCLUDE_SM_OBJ              /* shared memory objects (unbundled) */
```

A.1.45 SNMP Agent – add-on

VxWorks offers manageability through SNMP. This is possible through this agent. If you do not use SNMP, you should not include it.

```
INCLUDE_SNMPD               /* SNMP Agent */
```

Tornado 2 adds debug capabilities, with debug level.

```
INCLUDE_SNMPD_DEBUG   /* SNMP Agent debugging */
[...]
SNMP_TRACE_LEVEL      0  /* Must be >= 0 and <= 3 with higher */
                         /* values giving more info and 0     */
                         /* giving no info                    */
```

A.1.46 SPY, Task Monitoring Facility – default disabled

Spy was the old, pre-Tornado-*Browser* equivalent, offering periodical update information on the time spent in a specific task. Today, this is possible in a better way using the browser. If there is no target server, you may want this included, though.

```
INCLUDE_SPY                 /* spyLib for task monitoring */
```

A.1.47 Standalone Symbol table – default disabled

This switch should not be touched. The different *make*-targets exist for the different setups of the kernel, depending on the chosen target. So, you should not need to touch this at all. Do not do it.

```
INCLUDE_STANDALONE_SYM_TBL /* compiled-in symbol table */
```

A.1.48 Starting to do things right after booting, Startup Script – default disabled

Startup scripts are a convenient way of automatically executing commands after bootup, see chapter 4.1.1, page 46. To enable this feature, your target also needs the target-based shell and the target-based symbol table which allows the shell to look for the symbols called in the script.

Startup scripts originally are pre-Tornado tools.

```
INCLUDE_STARTUP_SCRIPT  /* execute start-up script */
```

A.1. VXWORKS MODULES

A.1.49 User-Readable Error states – default disabled

Another nice-to-have feature, which remains unused in production versions. Well that depends on whether you like it or not. Most of the time, simply ignore it.

```
INCLUDE_STAT_SYM_TBL    /* create user-readable error status */
```

A.1.50 Standard I/O – default

This definition should not be touched unless you definitely know what you are doing; you nearly always need it to be enabled.

```
INCLUDE_STDIO           /* standard I/O */
```

A.1.51 STREAMS – add-on

UNIX System V compatible STREAMS are another add-on package to help porting UNIX code to VxWorks. The different levels of compatibility can be enabled, depending on what you need or do not need.

```
INCLUDE_STREAMS          /* CORE Streams (stream head) */
INCLUDE_STREAMS_ALL      /* Complete Streams subsystem */
INCLUDE_STREAMS_AUTOPUSH /* SVR4 autopush mechanism */
INCLUDE_STREAMS_DEBUG    /* Streams Debugging facility */
INCLUDE_STREAMS_DLPI     /* Streams DLPI to mbuf compat. driver */
INCLUDE_STREAMS_SOCKET   /* Streams Socket layer & socket library */
INCLUDE_STREAMS_STRACE   /* Streams trace utility */
INCLUDE_STREAMS_STRERR   /* Streams error log utility */
INCLUDE_STREAMS_TLI      /* Streams TLI layer and TLI library */
DEFAULT_STREAMS_SOCKET   /* default to Streams socket for AF_INET */
```

Tornado 2 adds Routing Sockets to the setup above:

```
INCLUDE_ROUTE_SOCK       /* include routing socket interface */
```

A.1.52 Software Floating Point – default disabled as of Tornado 2

Do not touch it; it is a basic system feature that should be set by the BSP.

```
INCLUDE_SW_FP            /* software floating point emulation */
```

A.1.53 Symbol Table – default disabled

The Symbol-Table package originates from the pre-Tornado times of VxWorks. As people still like the possibility to keep the direct target access through the shell, there is also a need for the target-resident symbol table.

But, to allow parallel usage of *windsh*, the synchronization option is necessary to keep both symbol tables updated.

```
INCLUDE_SYM_TBL          /* symbol table package */
INCLUDE_SYM_TBL_SYNC     /* synch. host and target symbol tables */
```

A.1.54 Task Hooks - default

The package allows additional functions to be called whenever actions concerning tasks are executed, like rescheduling, creation and deletion (more common).

```
INCLUDE_TASK_HOOKS       /* include kernel callouts */
```

A.1.55 Task Variables – default

Task variables allow variables which are kept local to a task. Normally, all general variables are visible to all tasks, and static variables are kept the same within a source code module, even if it is executed in two different task contexts.

This is the way around that shortcoming.

```
INCLUDE_TASK_VARS        /* task variable package */
```

A.1.56 TCP Debug Tools – default disabled

A toolset to allow the debugging of TCP connections. Normally not necessary at all.

```
INCLUDE_TCP_DEBUG        /* TCP debug facility */
```

A.1.57 Telnet Style Remote Login to the target system – default disabled

This is the equivalent to rlogin, only for telnet. So, you also need a symbol table and shell included on the target system. Also remember to enable security.

```
INCLUDE_TELNET           /* telnet-style remote login */
```

A.1. VXWORKS MODULES   155

A.1.58 TFTP Tools – default disabled

These two definitions allow the usage of TFTP to transfer data.

```
INCLUDE_TFTP_CLIENT     /* tftp client */
INCLUDE_TFTP_SERVER     /* tftp server */
```

As of Tornado 2, the client has been enabled.

A.1.59 Function Execution Time Measurement Library – default

The **timex()** and **timexN()** commands allow the measurement of function execution time. This library should be discarded for the production system.

```
INCLUDE_TIMEX           /* timexLib for exec timing */
```

A.1.60 Serial Devices – default

The package allows the attachment of tty devices.

```
INCLUDE_TTY_DEV         /* attach serial drivers */
```

A.1.61 Object Module Unloader – default

The unloader is interesting as long as you need to load, debug and re-load object modules. Discard the library for production unless you need runtime reconfiguration capabilities.

```
INCLUDE_UNLOADER        /* object module unloading */
```

As of Tornado 2 the unloader has been disabled.

A.1.62 Watchdogs – default

Watchdog timers are important for most real-time applications. Beware, though, that this is purely software, not hardware-based!

```
INCLUDE_WATCHDOGS       /* include watchdogs */
```

A.1.63 WDB, the Wind DeBug Agent – default

The WDB is the target system instance of Tornado which manages the connection to all host systems. So, if you are interested in using the Tornado tools, keep it enabled.

Additionally, the WDB's mode can be pre-determined. `DUAL` is certainly the most usual, and safest choice.

```
INCLUDE_WDB               /* WDB debug agent */
INCLUDE_WDB_BANNER        /* print banner after agent starts */
INCLUDE_WDB_TTY_TEST      /* test serial line communication */
INCLUDE_WDB_VIO           /* virtual I/O support */

#define WDB_MODE WDB_MODE_DUAL /* WDB_MODE_[DUAL|TASK|EXTERN] */
```

Tornado 2 adds more config options – but remember they tell you not to touch them!

```
/* optional agent facilities */

INCLUDE_WDB_START_NOTIFY  /* notify the host of task creation */
INCLUDE_WDB_USER_EVENT    /* user events handling */

/* core agent facilities - do not remove */

INCLUDE_WDB_CTXT          /* context control */
INCLUDE_WDB_FUNC_CALL     /* spawn function as separate task */
INCLUDE_WDB_DIRECT_CALL   /* call function in agents context */
INCLUDE_WDB_EVENTS        /* host async event notification */
INCLUDE_WDB_GOPHER        /* gopher info gathering */
INCLUDE_WDB_BP            /* breakpoint support */
INCLUDE_WDB_EXC_NOTIFY    /* notify host of exceptions */
INCLUDE_WDB_EXIT_NOTIFY   /* notify the host of task exit */
INCLUDE_WDB_REG           /* get/set hardware registers */
INCLUDE_WDB_EVENTPOINTS   /* eventpoints handling */
INCLUDE_WDB_MEM           /* optional memory services */
```

A.1.64 Zero Copying Sockets – default disabled

Usually when using the IP stack, you data is copied two to three times before the packet is finally sent to the network. As this takes time, zero copy buffers are an alternative. They have a slightly different interface, though!

```
INCLUDE_ZBUF_SOCK         /* zbuf socket interface */
```

A.1.65 New features with Tornado 2 – default disabled

Tornado 2 has again added a wealth of features that has been left disabled.

General Options

They all stand for add-on product sets. Contact your FAE for specifics.

```
INCLUDE_HTML         /* include HTML support */
INCLUDE_JAVA         /* Java virtual machine */
INCLUDE_RBUFF        /* ring of buffers library */
INCLUDE_UGL          /* include Universal Graphic Library support */
INCLUDE_WILLOWS_RT   /* include Willows RT library */
INCLUDE_VXFUSION     /* WindMP (unbundled) */
```

Networking protocols

The new network stack also adds support for another set of protocols like OSPF and RIP. VxWorks could send RIP messages before[1], but not receive and act upon them.

SNTP, Simple Network Time Protocol allows you to get the system time from a network time server.

```
INCLUDE_OSPF         /* open shortest path first routing protocol */
INCLUDE_RIP          /* Routing Information Protocol RIP */

INCLUDE_SNTPC        /* SNTP client */
INCLUDE_SNTPS        /* SNTP server */
```

A.2 CPU Types

This section lists and shortly describes the different CPU types supported by VxWorks as currently available. For more current information, see the book's internet page.

A.2.1 MC68000, MC68010, MC68020, MC68030, MC68040, MC68LC040, MC68060 – Motorola 680x0 Series

68k is the "father" of 32 bit real time processors. It's successors still comprise a large part of the market place for real time systems. The PowerPC is intended to become the 68k successor as shown by Apple, but due to some design decisions, 68k still has its market.

A.2.2 CPU32 – Motorola MC 68360 Series

The 68360 is a mix of the processor core of the Motorola CPU-32+, accompanied by four Serial Controllers (SCCs).

---
[1] It normally would not, unless in some specific configurations, though

158   APPENDIX A. IMPORTANT DEFINES AND MODULES

A.2.3 SPARC, SPARClite – SUN Microsystems SPARC Architecture

The SPARC processor is a workstation processor which is also used in real time applications.
SPARClite support has been dropped as a single CPU type.

A.2.4 I960CA, I960KA, I960KB, I960JX, I960HX – Intel i960 CPU Series

i960, an Intel designed RISC processor series. Originally used in workstations, today it is used in embedded applications.

A.2.5 R3000, R4000, R4000, R4650, MIPS – MIPS Processors

The MIPS processor series has become base for a lot of workstation designs as well as a very common processor for embedded applications. So, this is how it is supported.
Tornado 2 now uses MIPS only.

A.2.6 AM29030, AM29200, AM29035 – AM29xxx Series

Older family of RISC processors.

A.2.7 PPC601, PPC602, PPC603, PPC604, PPC403. PPC505, PPC740, PPC750, PPC860, PPCEC603 – Motorola/IBM/Apple PowerPC Series

PowerPC, successor of the Motorola 680x0 Processor series.

A.2.8 I80386, I80486, I80X86 – Intel x86 Series

The PC processor is being used for desktop as well as embedded applications.

A.2.9 SIMSPARCSUNOS, SIMSPARCSOLARIS, SIMHPPAHPUX, SIMNT – VxWorks Simulator Pseudo-Processor Series

This simulator is a means of testing if you do not have the hardware available for whatever reason and enables you to start development even before actual hardware becomes available.

Appendix B

Makefile Rules — A Short Introduction

A real introduction to Makefiles can be found in [Tal91]. This section is intended to give a short overview of some basic principles of Makefiles.

Makefiles contain a set of rules to be used by the *make* program to aid in building applications which consist of several interdependent modules. Additionally, they offer the possibility to just type a single command instead of having to enter a long compiler command line every time when compiling.

This section contains examples and excerpts from a simple project. For this project size, normally, a makefile would be pure overkill; while debugging, though, makefiles can save a lot of typing.

For the examples in this document we will again use a PowerPC for the architecture.

This yields, according to Wind River's rules, the nomenclature <*UNIX-tool-name*> <*Architecture*>. E.g., the UNIX compiler is *cc*, the architecture is *ppc*, so we end up with *ccppc* as cross compiler for PowerPC. See table 2.1, page 13 for a detailed list.

B.1 Definitions And Rules

First of all, the makefile consists of a few definitions which may be used thereafter by the rules to enable *make* to build everything as defined.

These definitions set variables which then are used in the make process. Here, the definitions for the C Compiler (CC), the flags to pass on to the compiler (CFLAGS) and other settings are made. Additionally, groups can be created which keep some things together, like SRC, OBJ and TARGET below. An example could be:

```
CC      = ccppc
```

Based on these definitions, rules are built and then are carried out by *make*. Makefile rules have the following form:

```
TARGET   : DEPENDENCIES
           commands to execute
```

`TARGET` implies the items that need to be created. There are also general targets, like .c.o, meaning a xxx.c file, which is intended to be converted to a xxx.o file. Also, empty `DEPENDENCIES` are possible. Then the value needs to be replaced with a ";".

The `DEPENDENCY` refers to the items that are necessary to keep the target up to date, i.e. if something in `DEPENDENCY` changes, that the target needs to be recreated.

The `commands to execute` are the list of shell commands, including the variable substitution, which have to be executed to recreate the target.

B.1.1 Additional Standard Targets

Some additional targets should be part of any makefile. Namely, the target *clean* means that the source code directory is changed to a state where no intermediate files are left over, only the really essential files remain. E.g., all object modules and created files are removed as well as the editor's backup files etc.

Another target to be found everywhere is *all*. This is what *make* looks for when being called without any argument. When called with an argument, this argument is the target *make* looks for and tries to create.

Positive additional targets which may prove very important are *archive*, which may also be called *tar* and *depend*.

archive means 'create an archive out of the necessary files'. This should be set up and used if you want to re-distribute your source files or for archive purposes. It should automatically create an archive which contains all files necessary to work with your project. This will enable better backups, using just one command.

depend is the target to check the interdependencies of your files. This allows *make* to easily determine which files need recompilation, and which do not, thus speeding up your compile times. One important line (which you should obey) is:

```
# DO NOT DELETE THIS LINE -- makedepend depends on it.
```

It parts the main makefile part from the 'additional information' part. As it says — do not delete it! It is a great help and used by *makedepend*.

B.1.2 A Dependency Checker – *makedepend*

makedepend is a helper application which works like a C compiler. It takes C source code plus all include directives and checks which files the code uses through the `#include` preprocessor command. These dependencies are added to the end of the makefile as is visible below.

However, these days dependencies are created in *depend.<YOUR_BSP_NAME>* using *gcc*.

B.2 Example Codes

After all this theory, let us have a look at the real thing.

This section simply contains a makefile plus two example source codes to show the real/life variant of *make*.

Actually, this makefile is quite an overkill, because we only create one object module, which is then converted into a library. There might be a list of source and include file; then it would look as follows:

```
SRC     =       a.c \
                b.c
```

B.2.1 Example *Makefile*

```
#
# Definitions
#
CC       = ccppc
LD       = ldppc
INCLUDE  = -I$(WIND_BASE)/target/h
CFLAGS   = -DCPU=PPC604 -Wall -pedantic
OPTIM    = -O
DEBUG    = -g
SRC      = rtc.c
HDR      = rtc.h
OBJ      = rtc.o
TARGET   = rtc.a
#
# rules
#
all:     $(OBJ)
         $(LD) -o $(TARGET) -r $(OBJ)

.c.o:;
         $(CC) $(CFLAGS) $(OPTIM) $(DEBUG) $(INCLUDE) -c $*.c

clean:;
         rm -f *o *~ *a *bak *tar

archive: $(TARGET) $(OBJ)
         tar cvf rtc.tar $(SRC) $(HDR) $(OBJ) $(TARGET) Makefile

depend:;
         cp Makefile Makefile.bak;
         makedepend $(CFLAGS) $(INCLUDE) $(SRC)


# DO NOT DELETE THIS LINE -- makedepend depends on it.
rtc.o: (...)/Tornado/target/h/vxWorks.h
(...)
```

B.2.2 rtc.h

This is the include file for our little RTC (Real Time Clock) application. It creates nothing more than a small structure to allow readable code instead of lots of dangerous #defines.

```
typedef struct rtc
{
  volatile unsigned char
    rtc1sec,                    /* Second Digit */
    rtc10sec,                   /* 10 Seconds Digit */
    rtc1min,                    /* Minute Digit */
    rtc10min,                   /* 10 Minutes Digit */
    rtc1hr,                     /* Hour Digit */
    rtc10hr,                    /* 10 Hours Digit */
    rtc1day,                    /* Day Digit */
    rtc10day,                   /* 10 Days Digit */
    rtc1mon,                    /* Month Digit */
    rtc10mon,                   /* 10 Months Digit */
    rtc1yr,                     /* Year Digit */
    rtc10yr,                    /* 10 Year Digit */
    rtcweek,                    /* Week Number */
    rtcConD,                    /* Control Register D */
    rtcConE,                    /* Control Register E */
    rtcConF;                    /* Control Register F */
} RTC;
```

B.2.3 rtc.c

And this is the application. It does nothing more than read the RTC and print the values it reads whenever they change. Really simple!

The clock can only be read if disabled. That status is signaled with the busy bit that must not be set when reading. So, let us poll it after stopping the clock and re-enable the clock quickly after reading.

```
#include "vxWorks.h"
#include "sysLib.h"
#include "stdio.h"
#include "taskLib.h"

#include "rtc.h"

void rtc()
{
  RTC *clock=(RTC *)0xff803000;  /* Set base address (see manual!) */

  unsigned char busybit, oldvalue;
  unsigned char seconds=0, minutes=0, hours=0;

  while (1)
```

B.3. COMPILER OPTIONS

```
{
    clock->rtcConD |= 0x01;         /* set HOLD bit to 1 */
    busybit = clock->rtcConD;
    oldvalue = seconds;             /* memorize old value */

    if ((busybit & 0x02) != 0)      /* read BUSY bit */
    {
        clock->rtcConD &= 0xFE;     /* HOLD bit to 0 */
        taskDelay (1);              /* wait 190 us minimum */
    }
    else
    {
        seconds = (clock->rtc1sec & 0x0f);  /* read Seconds */
        seconds += (clock->rtc10sec & 0x0f )*10;
        minutes = (clock->rtc1min & 0x0f);  /* read Minutes */
        minutes += (clock->rtc10min & 0x0f)*10;
        hours   = (clock->rtc1hr & 0x0f);   /* read Hours */
        hours   += (clock->rtc10hr & 0x0f)*10;

        clock->rtcConD &= 0xFE;     /* HOLD bit to 0 */
    }

    if (oldvalue != seconds)        /* every second */
    {
        printf(" %d : %d : %d \n", hours, minutes, seconds);
    }
}
}
```

B.3 Compiler Options

Compiler options play an important role in selecting what and how modules are compiled. Thus, a few of the most important ones will be discussed here.

Additional information can be found in [FSF99b].

B.3.1 Compilation, Linking and Debugging

These are the most important options when compiling. To compile only, the option **-c** is used. this will yield an object module, with the suffix *.o*.

To add debug information which allows a symbolic, source level debugger to work with the object module, use the option **-g**.

Common Pitfalls

- Do not use the compiler to link your code!

  When using the compiler to link an object, it will try to create an executable. This is achieved by linking *libc.a* to the object modules, plus adding the pre-functions out of *crt0.o* (startup code) and the post-functions out of *crti.o* (cleanup code). As VxWorks does not need this and these files are not supplied, the link will fail. That is it.

- Do not name a function **main()**!
  When creating the function **main()**, compilers tend to create some additional helper code, callouts to some functions etc. So, without even making an error, you will see an error when downloading your program. Workaround? Simple: do not do it!

B.3.2 Optimization

Optimization is enabled using the compiler command line option *-O*. If this is not specified, the compiler will not optimize at all; this means, for variable transaction, that they are executed through memory accesses – no register optimization at all! *-O* yields a first, basic level of optimization, with register optimization and some additional functionality. Again, see the GCC User's manual for more specific information. Additional levels of optimization can be achieved using the optimization levels 1,2,3 and 6, i.e. *-O2*, *-O3*, *-O6*.

Warning! Optimization always means that the compiler has to make guesses about your goals. This may work but is not necessarily the case. So, make sure the code generated meets your program's intentions, but do not take it for granted. See page 126, chapter 8.2 for additional information.

Appendix C

Building you own Toolchain

The standard versions of the toolchain as delivered with VxWorks/Tornado normally lags slightly behind the publicly available GNU tools. Every now and then, you may need the additional features which are delivered with the new version, and when you do so, you need to ftp the new packages, recompile and run *them* instead of the ones delivered with Tornado.

For this case, we will show how to do so for a SPARC target system, building on Solaris 2.5. To achieve this, you need to configure your cross-compiling installation for this kind of setup. The way to specify a system type works as follows: GNU specifies these names according to a simple convention - *<Processor>-<vendor>-<operating system>*, e.g. *sparc-wrs-vxworks*, or *sparc-sun-solaris2.5*.

One warning should be issued: even though, normally, you are not bound to see any problems, this is of course not supported by Wind River nor anyone else, including me. You are pretty much on your own here!

Another new warning: gcc 2 and gcc 3 libraries have a different layout and can not be mixed. As WRS keep updating the compiler, you should ask your FAE whether something you believe to need is available or may be made available!

C.1 Getting the Files

The utilities you need, are:

- The GNU Compiler, package *gcc-*.tar.gz*

- The GNU Binutils, package *binutil*.tar.gz*

You can get these packages either from the GNU homepage, *www.gnu.org* or any mirror of the GNU archives.

C.2 Rebuilding the Complete Toolchain

The build consists of two parts, first the mandatory build of the latest *binutils* version, second the build of the *gcc*.

The configuration is performed using a standard GNU tool, called *configure*. To find out more about the options supported for the specific version, run `./configure --help`. If you need a different setup, you are free to select it. Additionally, you should read the files *README* and *INSTALL*, which are part of the package.

C.2.1 Building the Utility Toolchain

To build the tools, you first need to unpack the packages in a temporary place. Then, enter the directory which was unpacked and execute the configuration tool *configure*:

```
% ./configure --prefix=YOUR_INSTALLATION_BASE_DIRECTORY
   --target=sparc-wrs-vxworks
(... output deleted)
% make
```

The next step is to install it all:

```
% make install
(... output deleted)
```

Now, the toolchain except the compiler has been installed!

C.2.2 Rebuilding *gcc*

To be able to make *gcc*, you also need the VxWorks include files. Copy them to the target directory as follows - if you do not need them here afterwards, make sure to save a backup copy of the *include* directory so you can restore it later!

```
% cp -r $(WIND_BASE)/target/h
   YOUR_INSTALLATION_BASE_DIRECTORY/sparc-wrs-vxworks/include
%
```

Finally, you can now configure and make your compiler.

```
% ./configure --prefix=YOUR_INSTALLATION_BASE_DIRECTORY
   --target=sparc-wrs-vxworks
(... output deleted)
% make LANGUAGES="c c++ protoize"
(lots of output omitted)
% make LANGUAGES="c c++ protoize" install
(installation output moitted)
```

This builds and installs the compiler for C, C++ and for an additional tool called *protoize* which allows to convert K&R C code to ANSI C code and vice versa.

Appendix D

Pointers to Different Internet Sites

This is a completely biased, personal list of interesting Internet sites which will probably prove far from complete. Anyway, you should use this list as a starting point for finding further information.

D.1 Specifications And References Online

This lists some exemplary sites which carry online versions of the most important specifications. Be warned, as the web changes rapidly, these sites may have moved to different places already. Nevertheless, this may be a starting point for research.

Organization	Topic	Address
VITA	VME	*www.vita.com*
PCI Manufacturers	CompactPCI, CompactTCA, AdvancedTCA	*www.picmg.com*
PCI Special Interest Group	PCI Bus	*www.pcisig.com*
Intel Processor Documentation	i960, x86, XScale	*www.intel.com*
Motorola Processor Documentation	PowerPC, 68k	*www.motorola.com*
GroupIPC	Mezzanine Modules and Manufacturers	*www.groupipc.com*
NSSN	National Standard Search Engine – ANSI etc.	*www.nssn.org*
IEEE	IEEE Internet Site	*www.ieee.org*
The Landfield Group	References	*www.landfield.com*
Merriam Webster Co	WWWebster	*www.m-w.com*
Dinkum C Reference	ANSI C Standard Documentation	*www.dinkumware.com/refxc.html*

D.2 Online VxWorks Pages And General Real-time Related Information

Organization	Address
Wind River Systems	www.wrs.com
WindRiver Developer Network	developer.windriver.com
Dedicated Systems Journal and Encyclopedia	www.realtime-info.be
Embedded Systems Resources	www.eg3.com/real/index.htm and www.eg3.com/realv/index.htm
VxWorks FTP Archive (old, yet interesting)	ftp://ftp.atd.ucar.edu/pub/archive/vxworks
Tornado II FAQ	www.xs4all.nl/~borkhuis/vxworks/vxworks.html
More VxWorks FAQs	www.faqs.org/faqs/vxworks-faq
VxWorks Experiments	www.rt.db.erau.edu/experiments/vx/toc/TableOfContents.htm

D.3 Programming Tools Online

Organization	Address
Free Software Foundation (GNU Project)	www.gnu.org
Cygnus Inc., now a subsidiary of RedHat Inc.	www.cygnus.com
Interesting and Useful projects at RedHat Inc.	sources.redhat.com
SourceNavigator is a free Sniff look-alike	snavigator.sourceforge.net
Greenhills Software Homepage	www.ghi.com
Shareware Servers	www.cdrom.com, www.download.com and many more

D.4 Newsgroups

If you do not have access to a news server, use *groups.google.com* to read them.

Newsgroup	Description
comp.os.vxworks	VxWorks Exploder Gatewayed Newsgroup (i.e. Postings to the Newsgroup appear on the mailinglist *vxw-explo@lbl.gov* and vice versa)
comp.realtime	General realtime-related newsgroup
comp.arch.bus.vmebus	VMEbus related Newsgroup (very few postings)
comp.sys.m68k	680x0 Processor Series related Newsgroup
comp.sys.intel	Intel Processor related Newsgroup
comp.sys.powerpc.*	PowerPC Related Newsgroup hierarchy
comp.sys.sun.hardware	SPARC hardware related Newsgroup
comp.sys.arm	ARM RISC Related Newsgroup
comp.sys.m88k	88xxx Processor family related Newsgroup
comp.sys.mips	MIPS Ryx000 Processor family related Newsgroup

D.5 This Book

For comments, corrections or questions, you can always reach the author at his private email address *Christof.Wehner@christofwehner.de*. This account cannot be checked daily, so there may be a short delay in answering any questions.

Additionally, there may be more information plus these (more or less regularly updated) links at *www.christofwehner.de*.

Index

.wind, 36

additional documentation, 20
addressing, 73
Architecture Supplement, 20
architecture, layered, 9

backplane, IP address, 44
BAT, 74
batch file to install Tornado 1/VxWorks 5.2 BSP for Windows, 28
big endian, 73
binutils, 11
board support package, 10
boot device, 42
boot file, 44
boot flash, 46
boot from SCSI device, 48
boot parameters, 41
boot PROM, 46
bootChange(), 39
bootConfig.c, 122
bootrom, 39, 41, 46, 122
bootrom code, 122
bootrom, parameters, 41
bootrom.hex, 39
bootrom_uncmp, 39
bridge, 75
bridge caveats, 80
browser, 15
BSD 4.3, 101
BSP, 10
BSP documentation, 21
BSP installation, 27
BSP installation, manual, 29
bus devices, 73

bus devices, programming, 77

C++, 69, 94
C++ support, 141
C++, iostreams, 141
C++, tools.h++, 141
C++, Wind Foundation Classes, 141
caveats, compilers and structures, 79
caveats, access accumulation, 80
caveats, bridge, 80
caveats, Compiler, 79
caveats, out-of-order execution, 79
caveats, PPC, 79
choosing include files, 63
Clock, Real Time, 96
coding conventions, 93
commands, built-in, 34
commands, target shell, 34
Compact PCI WWW site, 167
CompactPCI, 89
Compiler caveats, 79
Compiler versions, 165
config directory, 30, 32
config.h, 34
configAll.h, 32, 37, 139
configuration, 59
configuration tool, 15, 59
configure, 166
conventions, coding, 93
CPCI, 89
CPCI slave address, 42
cpu types, 157
cpu types, '360, 157
cpu types, 68k, 157
cpu types, AM29xxx, 158
cpu types, i960, 158

INDEX

cpu types, MIPS, 158
cpu types, PowerPC, 158
cpu types, QUICC, 157
cpu types, simulator, 158
cpu types, SPARC, 158
cpu types, x86, 158
cross development, 9
crosswind, 15, 17, 67
Customer Support User's Guide, 20
Cygnus Inc., 11, 168

debug low level programs, 79
debug tools, WindView, 144
debugging techniques, 66
debugging using H/W breakpoints, 68
debugging, printf(), 66
debugging, using a debugger, 67
DEC 21140, 113
default user, 69
defs.$(WIND_HOST_TYPE), 106
defs.bsp, 106
descriptor, device, 78
determinism, 7
development, cross, 9
development, target based, 8
device descriptor, 78
device initialization function, 78
device probing, 78
device programming, 77
device programming, trouble shooting, 79
device structure, 78
DNS, 43
docs directory, 31
documentation, additional, 20
documentation, Architecture Supplement, 20
documentation, BSP, 21
documentation, Customer Support User's Guide, 20
documentation, ELAN, 20
documentation, GNU toolset, 20
documentation, online, 21

documentation, printing, 21
documentation, Tornado API guide, 20
documentation, Tornado User's Guide, 19
documentation, VxWorks Network Programmer's Guide, 19
documentation, VxWorks Programmer's Guide, 19
documentation, VxWorks Programmer's Reference, 19
dosFsMkfs(), 53
drivers, 92
dynamic startup, 71

edge sensitive interrupts, 88
ELAN directory, 36
ELAN documentation, 20
Embedded Tools, RedHat, 168
encapsulation, hardware, 92
endian-ness, 73, 77, 92
errno, 25
example makefile, 161
execution time measurement, 155

fields of sysPhysMemDesc, 73
floating point libraries, 143
formatted I/O, 144
Free Software Foundation, 168
ftp server, 144

gateway, IP address, 44
gcc, 11
gcc version 3, 165
gcc version conflict, 165
gdb, 15, 17
GNU naming convention, 165
GNU project, 168
GNU toolset documentation, 20
Greenhills Software Inc., 168

h directory, 32
hardware encapsulation, 92
host, 5
host directory, 31

INDEX

host, IP address, 44
hostname, 43

I/O system, 145
i960 WWW site, 167
ide, 14
IEEE WWW site, 167
include directory, 32
include file selection, 63
initialization function, for a device, 78
inline declaration, 78
installation problems, 28
installing BSPs, 27
installing Tornado 1/VxWorks 5.2 BSPs
  in Windows, 28
installOption, 28
intconnect(), 88
interrupt mode, SM network, 114
interrupt number, 86
interrupt sensitivity, 88
interrupt service routine, 85
interrupt vector, 86, 88, 89
interrupts, 85, 88
interrupts, edge sensitive, 88
interrupts, level sensitive, 88
iostreams, 141
IP address, backplane, 44
IP address, gateway, 44
IP address, host, 44
IP address, target system, 44
IRQ, 88
IRQ sensitivity, 88
ISR, 85

kernel types, 38
kernel, general, 10

layered architecture, 9
level sensitive interrupts, 88
libraries, floating point, 143
license directory, 36
licensing info, 27
linking code, 65
little endian, 73

LM_LICENSE_PATH, 36
loader, 145
location monitor, 87
logging, 145
login, 45
loginUserAdd(), 144
logMsg(), 144, 145
low level programming, 77
low level programs, debugging, 79

mailbox, 87
mailbox mode, SM network, 115
make, 18
make targets, 38
makedepend, 160
Makefile, 18
Makefile definitions, 159
Makefile dependencies, 160
Makefile rules, 159
makefile, example, 161
Makefiles, 159
Manual Installation, 29
master window, 75, 111
master window - PowerCore setup, 75
measurement, function execution time,
  155
memDesc.c, 73
Memory Management Unit, 73
memory manager, 145
memory map, 73
mib 2, 145
MMU, 73, 74
mmu support, 146
modules, 139

network, 101
network addresses, 58
network, shared memory, 57
networking, 146
networking module, 101
NFS, 147
NFS client, 147
NFS mount all command, 147

INDEX

NFS Server, 147
NMI, 90
NMI, return from, 90
Non Maskable Interrupts, 90

object module unloader, 155
object module loader, 145
Object Oriented Programming, 94
online documentation, 21
online specifications, 167
OOx, 94

password, default, 69
password, FTP boot, 45
password, protection, 69
PCI WWW site, 167
PMC WWW site, 167
polling mode, SM network, 114
portability, 7, 9, 90
POSIX, 95
POSIX modules, 148
PowerCore VME window setup, 75
PowerPC WWW site, 167
PPC caveats, 79
PPP, 148
predictability, 7
printErr(), 25
printf(), 144
printf() debugging, 66
printing man pages, 21
prjParams.h, 37
problems, common, 60
problems, installation, 28
processor number, 42
profiling, 128
programming bus devices, 77
programming, low level, 77
Programming, Object Oriented, 94
project tool, 16, 59
PROXY access, 148
PROXY ARP, 148
pSysScsiCtrl, 50

ram disk, 149

ramdrv, 149
Read-Modify-Write, 113
Real Time Clock, 96
real-time, 5
rebuilding the toolchain, 165
RedHat Inc., 168
register structure, 78
registry, 14
rlogin, 149
rlogin, security, 150
RMW, 113
router, 44
routing, 58
rsh, possible problems, 45
RTC – Real Time Clock, 96
rules.bsp, 32, 38–40, 60

S Record, 38
Script, Startup, 46
SCSI boot, 48
SCSI bootdisk setup, 50
SCSI, configuration, 120
scsiFormatUnit(), 53
select(), 93
SENS, 43
Shared Memory Network, 42, 57, 101, 113, 151
Shared Memory Objects, 152
shareware, 168
shell built-in commands, 34
Slave Address, 42
slave window, 42, 76, 111
sm boot device, 42, 57
sm Network, 42, 101, 113
SM network, interrupt mode, 114
SM network, mailbox mode, 115
SM network, polling mode, 114
SM_IT, 114
SM_MBOX, 115
SM_OFF_BOARD, 57, 118
SM_OFF_BOARD, when to use, 118
SM_POLL, 114
smNet, 57, 101

Source Navigator, 168
specifications online, 167
SREC, 38
STANDALONE_NET, 39, 60
standards conformance, 91
Standards Search Engine WWW site, 167
Startup Script, 46, 71
startup, dynamic, 71
static descriptor, 78
STREAMS, 81
structure, device registers, 78
symbol table, 154
symbol table synchronization, 154
symbol table, target resident, 154
sysLib.c, 73
sysPhysMemDesc, 73
sysPhysMemDesc fields, 73

Table Walk, MMU, 74
target, 5
target based development, 8
target directory, 32
target server, 14
target server licensing, 27
target, IP address, 44
target-resident symbol table, 154
TAS, 113
Test And set, 113
tgtsvr, 27
timer, watchdog, 155
timex, 155
timexN, 155
tLogTask, 145
toolchain, rebuilding, 165
tools.h++, 141
Tornado, 5
Tornado API Guide, 20
Tornado User's Guide, 19

unld(), 155
unloader, object modules, 155
user name, 45

usrExtra.c, 34
usrLib.c, 34
usrNetInit(), 39
usrNetwork.c, 34
usrScsi.c, 34

vector, interrupt, 88, 89
vi editor keys, 68
VITA WWW site, 167
VMEbus master window, 75, 111
VMEbus slave address, 42, 111
VMEbus slave window, 76
vwModNum.h, 25
VxMP, 57, 152
VxVMI, 110, 146
VxWorks, 5, 39
VxWorks Network Programmer's Guide, 19
VxWorks Programmer's Guide, 19
VxWorks Programmer's Reference, 19
vxWorks.st, 39
vxWorks.st_rom, 40, 60
vxWorks.st_rom.uncmp, 40, 60
vxWorks.sym, 39
vxWorks_rom, 39, 60

watchdog timer, 87, 155
wdb, 17, 156
Web Dictionary, 167
Web References, 167
When to use SM_OFF_BOARD, 118
Wind Foundation Classes, 69, 141
Wind River Systems WWW site, 168
windman, 21
window, master, 75
window, slave, 76
Windows Tornado 1/VxWorks 5.2 BSP installation script, 28
windsh, 14, 17, 149
WindView, 144
WindView instrumentation, 144
WP enable/disable, 111, 112
write posting, 111, 112

INDEX

x86 web site, 167
XScale web site, 167

Printed in the United Kingdom
by Lightning Source UK Ltd.
115986UKS00001B/95